Algorithmic Ethics

This book focuses on how new technologies are raising and reshaping ethical questions and practices that aim to automate ethics into program outputs.

With new powerful technologies come enhanced capacities to act, which in turn require new ethical concepts for guiding just and fair actions in the use of these new capabilities. The new algorithmic regimes, for their ethical articulation, build on prior ethics discourses in computer and information ethics, as well as the philosophical traditions of ethics generally. Especially as our technologies become more autonomous, operating alongside us in the home, workplace or on the roads, ethics has the potential to limit negative effects and shape the new technical terrain in a more humanly recognizable way. The volume covers a critique of human-centered AI, the effects of AI and the Internet of Things in the domain of human resource management, how decentralized finance applications on the blockchain encode ethical norms into "smart contracts," and the personal surveillance risks of audio beacon technology operating invisibly in our cellphones.

Scholars and students from many backgrounds, as well as policy makers, journalists and the general reading public, will find a multidisciplinary approach to questions posed by research in algorithmic ethics from the fields of management, sociology, social policy, public service, religion and interactive media.

Michael Filimowicz is Senior Lecturer in the School of Interactive Arts and Technology (SIAT) at Simon Fraser University. He has a background in computer-mediated communications, audiovisual production, new media art and creative writing. His research develops new multimodal display technologies and forms, exploring novel form factors across different application contexts including gaming, immersive exhibitions and simulations.

Algorithms and Society

Series Editor

Dr Michael Filimowicz

Senior Lecturer in the School of Interactive Arts and Technology (SIAT) at Simon Fraser University.

As algorithms and data flows increasingly penetrate every aspect of our lives, it is imperative to develop sufficient theoretical lenses and design approaches to humanize our informatic devices and environments. At stake are the human dimensions of society which stand to lose ground to calculative efficiencies and performance, whether at the service of government, capital, criminal networks, or even a general mob concatenated in social media.

Algorithms and Society is a new series which takes a broad view of the information age. Each volume focuses on an important thematic area, from new fields such as software studies and critical code studies to more established areas of inquiry such as philosophy of technology and science and technology studies. This series aims to stay abreast of new areas of controversy and social issues as they emerge with the development of new technologies.

If you wish to submit a book proposal for the series, please contact Dr Michael Filimowicz michael_f@sfu.ca or Emily Briggs emily.briggs@tandf.co.uk

Algorithmic Ethics
Algorithms and Society
Edited by Michael Filimowicz

China's Digital Civilization
Algorithms and Society
Edited by Michael Filimowicz

Decolonizing Data
Algorithms and Society
Edited by Michael Filimowicz

Information Disorder
Algorithms and Society
Edited by Michael Filimowicz

For more information on the series, visit: www.routledge.com/Algorithms-and-Society/book-series/ALGRAS

Algorithmic Ethics

Algorithms and Society

Edited by Michael Filimowicz

LONDON AND NEW YORK

First published 2023
by Routledge
4 Park Square, Milton Park, Abingdon, Oxon OX14 4RN

and by Routledge
605 Third Avenue, New York, NY 10158

Routledge is an imprint of the Taylor & Francis Group, an informa business

British Library Cataloguing-in-Publication Data
A catalogue record for this book is available from the British Library

Library of Congress Cataloging-in-Publication Data
Names: Filimowicz, Michael, editor.
Title: Algorithmic ethics : algorithms and society / edited by Michael Filimowicz.
Description: Abingdon, Oxon ; New York, NY : Routledge, 2023. | Series: Algorithms and society | Includes bibliographical references and index.
Identifiers: LCCN 2023009465 (print) | LCCN 2023009466 (ebook) | ISBN 9781032290652 (hardback) | ISBN 9781032290669 (paperback) | ISBN 9781003299882 (ebook)
Subjects: LCSH: Technological innovations—Moral and ethical aspects. | Information technology—Moral and ethical aspects. | Technological innovations—Social aspects. | Information technology—Social aspects.
Classification: LCC BJ59 .A43 2024 (print) | LCC BJ59 (ebook) | DDC 170—dc23/eng/20230419
LC record available at https://lccn.loc.gov/2023009465
LC ebook record available at https://lccn.loc.gov/2023009466

ISBN: 978-1-032-29065-2 (hbk)
ISBN: 978-1-032-29066-9 (pbk)
ISBN: 978-1-003-29988-2 (ebk)

DOI: 10.4324/9781003299882

Typeset in Times New Roman
by Apex CoVantage, LLC

Contents

Tables

Contributors

Jim Arrowsmith is Professor in the School of Management, Massey University (Auckland, New Zealand), where he teaches strategic and international HRM. He has published more than 60 articles in leading international journals in these areas. He is co-editor-in-chief of *Labour and Industry: A Journal of the Social and Economic Relations of Work*; is Associate Editor of the *International Journal of Human Resource Management* and *Service Business: An International Journal*; and is on the editorial boards of *Human Resource Management Journal*, *Industrial Relations Journal* and *Employee Relations*. He has acted as a consultant for the ILO advising Pacific Island countries on regulatory capacity and labor law reform.

Julian Iliev is currently a Ph.D. student in the School of Interactive Arts and Technology (SIAT) at Simon Fraser University. His Master of Arts research focused on the prevalence of audio beacon technologies and their implications for contemporary society.

Andreas Langenohl is Professor of Sociology at Justus Liebig University Giessen, Germany, and Professor Extraordinary of Political Studies at North-West University, South Africa. His research covers the social studies of finance, economic sociology, social and cultural theory, and transnationalism studies. His recent publications include "Safe assemblages: Thinking Infrastructures Beyond Circulation in the Times of SARS-CoV2," *Journal of International Relations and Development* (2021, with Carola Westermeier); "Securing the Separation Between State and Finance: Entanglements Between Securitization and Societal Differentiation," *Review of International Political Economy* (2021); "Algorithmic Reflexivity: The Constitution of Socio-technical Accountability in Financial Pricing," *Historical Social Research* (2021).

Johnny Långstedt is a grant writer at Åbo Akademi University (Turku, Finland). He has a Ph.D. in the study of religions. His research revolves around values and diversity in working life, the cultural consequences of AIS, change management and intercultural encounters in international construction projects.

Tamás Tóth is Assistant Professor at the University of Public Service. His research interests include populist political communication styles, journalism studies and academic knowledge production. Recently, he elaborated the content analysis refinements of explicit and implicit populism to scrutinize manifest and latent dichotomies in populist political communication. He has published in journals such as the *International Journal of Communication*, the *Journal of Contemporary European Studies*, the *European Journal of Science and Theology* and *Scientometrics*.

Lilla Vicsek, Ph.D., is Associate Professor at Corvinus University of Budapest. Her work for over a decade has focused on issues related to science and society, with publications appearing in journals such as *Science as Culture*, *New Genetics and Society*, *Science Communication* and the *Journal of Sociology*. Currently, her main research focus is the constitutive role of expectations regarding artificial intelligence. She is especially interested in how these expectations are related to ethics and power issues.

Series Preface

Algorithms and Society

Michael Filimowicz

This series is less about what algorithms are and more about how they act in the world through "eventful" (Bucher, 2018, p. 48) forms of "automated decision making" (Noble, 2018, loc. 141) in which computational models are "based on choices made by fallible human beings" (O'Neil, 2016, loc. 126).

> Decisions that used to be based on human refection are now made automatically. Software encodes thousands of rules and instructions computed in a fraction of a second.
>
> (Pasquale, 2015, loc. 189)

> If, in the industrial era, the promise of automation was to displace manual labor, in the information age it is to pre-empt agency, spontaneity, and risk: to map out possible futures before they hap-pen so objectionable ones can be foreclosed and desirable ones selected.
>
> (Andrejevic, 2020, p. 8)

> [M]achine learning algorithms that anticipate our future propensities are seriously threatening the chances that we have to make possible alternative political futures.
>
> (Amoore, 2020, p. xi)

Algorithms, definable pragmatically as "a method for solving a problem" (Finn, 2017, loc. 408), "leap from one feld to the next" (O'Neil, 2016, loc. 525). They are "hyperobjects: things with such broad temporal and spatial reach that they exceed the phenomenological horizon of human subjects" (Hong, 2020, p. 30). While in the main, the technological systems taken up as volume topics are design solutions to problems for which there are commercial markets, organized communities, or claims of state interest, their power and ubiquity generate new problems for inquiry. The series will do its part to track this domain fuidity across its volumes and contest, through critique and investigation, their "logic of secrecy" (Pasquale, 2015, loc. 68), and "obfuscation" (loc. 144).

These new social (rather than strictly computational) problems that are generated can, in turn, be taken up by many critical, policy, and speculative discourses. At their most productive, such debates can potentially alter the ethical, legal, and even imaginative parameters of the environments in which the algorithms of our information architectures and infrastructures operate, as algorithmic implementations often reflect a "desire for epistemic purity, of knowledge stripped of uncertainty and human guesswork" (Hong, 2020, p. 20). The series aims to foster a general intervention in the conversation around these often "black boxed" technologies and track their pervasive effects in society.

> Contemporary algorithms are not so much transgressing settled societal norms as establishing new patterns of good and bad, new thresholds of normality and abnormality, against which actions are calibrated.
>
> (Amoore, 2020, p. 5)

Less "hot button" algorithmic topics are also of interest to the series, such as their use in the civil sphere by citizen scientists, activists, and hobbyists, where there is usually not as much discursive attention. Beyond private, state, and civil interests, the increasingly sophisticated technology-based activities of criminals, whether amateur or highly organized, deserve broader attention as now everyone must defend their digital identities. The information systems of companies and states conduct a general form of "ambient surveillance" (Pasquale, 2015, loc. 310), and anyone can be a target of a hacking operation.

Algorithms and Society thus aims to be an interdisciplinary series which is open to researchers from a broad range of academic back-grounds. While each volume has its defined scope, chapter contributions may come from many areas such as sociology, communications, critical legal studies, criminology, digital humanities, economics, computer science, geography, computational media and design, philosophy of technology, and anthropology, along with others. Algorithms are "shaping the conditions of everyday life" (Bucher, 2018, p. 158) and operate "at the intersection of computational space, cultural systems, and human cognition" (Finn, 2017, loc. 160), so the multidisciplinary terrain is vast indeed. Since the series is based on the shorter Routledge Focus format, it can be nimble and responsive to emerging areas of debate in fast-changing technological domains and their sociocultural impacts.

References

Amoore, L. (2020). *Cloud ethics: Algorithms and the attributes of ourselves and others*. Duke University Press.

Andrejevic, M. (2020). *Automated media*. Taylor and Francis.

Bucher, T. (2018). *If. . . then: Algorithmic power and politics*. Oxford University Press.

Finn, E. (2017). *What algorithms want: Imagination in the age of computing* (Kindle Version). MIT Press.

Hong, S. H. (2020). *Technologies of speculation: The limits of knowledge in a data-driven society*. New York University Press.

Noble, S. U. (2018). *Algorithms of oppression* (Kindle Version). New York University Press.

O'Neil, C. (2016). *Weapons of math destruction* (Kindle Version). Broadway Books.

Pasquale, F. (2015). *The black box society* (Kindle Version). Harvard University Press.

Volume Introduction

With new powerful technologies come enhanced capacities to act, which in turn require new ethical concepts for guiding just and fair actions in the use of these new capabilities. The new algorithmic regimes, for their ethical articulation, build on prior ethics discourses in computer and information ethics, as well as the philosophical traditions of ethics generally. Especially as our technologies become more autonomous, operating alongside us in the home, workplace or on the roads, ethics has the potential to limit negative effects and shape the new technical terrains in a more humanly recognizable way.

Chapter 1—"Visions of Human-Centered Artificial Intelligence—Relations with Ethics and Power" by Lilla Vicsek and Tamás Tóth—unpacks the concept of "human-centered AI," which is gaining in popularity. AI ethics have become more prominent in recent years, inspiring many new AI approaches, many of which, like the idea of "human-centered AI," are conceptually and operationally flawed. First, this new concept tends to frame humanity monolithically, arguing that all societies face the same challenges. Second, human-centered AI is seen as primarily serving the Global North. Finally, capitalist system disparities are hardly discussed in the institutions under study.

Chapter 2—"Values, Work and Well-being in Artificial Intelligence Society: Exacerbating Dilemmas in Human Resource Management"' by Johnny Långstedt and James Arrowsmith—shows how AI and the "Internet of Things" are transforming work. New intelligent technologies will change industry logic, making labor uncertain for many while generating wealth for the few. Workplace changes have major cultural and organizational effects as they can increase worker stress and human resource management tensions, affecting well-being and forcing major operational changes throughout businesses and society.

Chapter 3—"In the Forefront of Code: Ethics in Decentralized Finance" by Andreas Langenohl—explores how DeFi and blockchain technologies reject assumptions about human trust and norm-obedient behavior, offering technological solutions to financial coordination challenges and using platforms to encode norm-obedient behavior. The chapter analyzes the ethical consequences using Michel Foucault's conception of ethics as distinct from morality and norm-obedience. That view sees ethics as a reflection on moral self-conduct before moral or technical code.

Chapter 4—"Audio Beacon Technologies, Surveillance and the Digital Paradox" by Julian Iliev–discusses audio beacon technologies in our cellphones and their consequences for individuals in contemporary society. This technology's concealed surveillance is investigated through the privacy literature and George Orwell's novel *1984*. This author recommends two general strategies to limit audio beacons' harmful effects: (1) immediate individual actions and (2) long-term government legislation to improve privacy. This research intends to increase public knowledge, which is needed for both solutions.

Acknowledgment

The chapter summaries here are in places drawn from the authors' chapter abstracts, the full versions of which can be found in Routledge's online reference for the volume.

Michael Filimowicz

contexts, using Michel Foucault's concept of the [illegible] morality and [illegible] view [illegible] self-[illegible]

Chapter 7 – [illegible] the [illegible] technologies in our [illegible] phones and [illegible] for individuals in contemporary society [illegible] technology's [illegible] surveillance [illegible] and George Orwell's 1984. The author recommends two [illegible] strategies to [illegible] (1) immediate individual [illegible] and (2) long-term [illegible] legislation to improve privacy. This [illegible] for both [illegible]

Acknowledgement

This chapter summarises [illegible] from the authors' chapter [illegible] [illegible] for their contributions.

Michael Friedewald

1 Visions of Human-Centered Artificial Intelligence

Relations with Ethics and Power

Lilla Vicsek and Tamás Tóth

Introduction

There has been heightened attention to the disruptive potentials of AI solutions and ethical issues lately. Leading companies in AI development have also begun to deal with ethical problems. However, the way they and other organizations have treated these has received severe criticism from social scientists. It seems ethics statements often serve the purpose of calming critical voices and reassuring the public, investors and legislators while deflecting regulation of the sphere (Kerr et al., 2020). Additionally, ethical discourses often cannot influence AI development and decision-making to a high degree as ethical considerations tend to be too general and not concrete enough for effective application (Kerr et al., 2020; Hagendorff, 2020).

Greene et al. (2019) have pointed out that high-profile ethical statements of major independent organizations between 2015 and 2018 did not question the "status quo": the current social and business arrangements under which AI was developed. This was typical of the statements, despite the fact that mainly huge companies without proper "democratic oversight" and with an underpaid, insecure workforce develop these technologies (Greene et al., 2019). Other activists and social scientists (Dotson, 2015) have claimed that the development of a profit-oriented technology does not always lead to the best solutions for humanity and could be harmful, especially if it is not regulated strongly enough.

Several authors have criticized the principles and values in ethical statements on AI as often representing Western neoliberal principles only and that, in applying them, they can contribute to global inequality (Stark et al., 2021; Monahan, 2021). Monahan (2021) has criticized the transparency ideal, especially in the case of surveillance, as contributing to the solidifying of Western white male supremacy. He argues, based on Haraway (1991), that science has often been tied to militarism, capitalism, colonialism and male supremacy. Much research in Science and Technology Studies (STS) has demonstrated how technological solutions often serve certain social goals of a specific privileged groups. Authors in STS often emphasize there are choices regarding

DOI: 10.4324/9781003299882-1

technological directions, and the resulting solutions can benefit some groups while not benefiting others. Moreover, the funds allocated to technological development are taking money away from other ways to help solve social problems.

Hagendorff (2020) has found in his analysis of 22 ethical guidelines that frequently mentioned aspects—such as accountability, explainability, privacy, justice, robustness and safety—were often executed as technical solutions. Based on Gilligan (1982), he asserts these technical solutions can be regarded as instances of male-dominated calculating and logic-oriented ethics, and the guidelines leave out non-masculine ways of thinking, including discussing AI ethics from the aspects of care, nurture, help, welfare, social responsibility and so on. "In AI ethics, technical artifacts are primarily seen as isolated entities that can be optimized by experts so as to find technical solutions for technical problems" (Hagendorff, 2020, p. 112). He found that even in the field of AI ethics, most authors are men, and that the problem of lack of diversity of AI developers is missing from many guidelines.

One term that has appeared to defend AI against criticisms is "human-centered AI." Projects and research centers use the term in their names. Additionally, university courses, MSc programs, companies, blogs refer to human-centered AI and EU Horizons mentions it as a priority. Therefore, we find it relevant to analyze visions of human-centered AI. We aim to examine visions of human-centered artificial intelligence (HAI); what these visions leave out and what they include, responding sensitively to issues of power and inequality within and between societies. We compare these visions with features of previous ethical value statements and guidelines. We also discuss the consequences of these expectations.

Our study is built on the following premises of the sociology of technological expectations: (1) anticipations of technologies are important aspects of modern capitalism (Beckert, 2016), (2) visions of technologies have a constitutive role as they can influence action, legitimize, show direction and coordinate actions of actors (Van Lente, 2012), (3) powerful actors can influence future expectations in science and technologies and thus shape the future by trying to marginalize alternative channels of future development (Brown et al., 2017). In this light, we investigate the HAI imaginaries of specific agents, namely university "institutes" to introduce their understanding of HAI concerning national and supranational levels.[1]

Methodology

Our goal was to analyze five university institutions' visions of HAI from the Global North (Demeter, 2020); therefore, we conducted qualitative, thematic content analysis on texts published via their official websites. We scrutinized

Table 1.1 Analyzed university's HAI institutes or research areas

University	*Institute*	*Hosting country*	*Text no. and share of the sample*
University of Bologna	Alma Mater Research Institute for Human-Centered Artificial Intelligence	Italy	n = 32 (5.6%)
Utrecht University	Human-centered Artificial Intelligence focus area	Netherlands	n = 59 (10.3%)
Stanford University	Institute for Human-Centered AI	United States	n = 352 (61.4%)
Northwestern University	Center for Human–Computer Interaction + Design, Human-Centered AI research area	United States	n = 36 (6.3%)
University of Maryland	Human-Computer Interaction Laboratory, Human-Centered AI research area	United States	n = 94 (16.4%)

five institutes (see Table 1.1) from two European and three American universities with "Human-centered" and "AI" terms in their names.

Our database consists of the institutions' introductions, goals, visions, staff biographies, published events, lectures, seminars, news, reports, interviews, calls for papers and grants. Note that as the extended reports published via Stanford University's website were extraordinarily long, we scrutinized only their introductions and conclusions. The total number of analyzed documents is 573. We started the data collection on July 6, 2021, and finished it on October 6, 2021, starting with the first published content from 2018.

In our scrutiny, we operationalized the following definition for a theme: it "captures something important about the data in relation to the research question, and represents some level of patterned response or meaning within the data set" (Braun & Clarke, 2006, p. 82). We analyzed the database using theoretical thematic analysis that primarily relied on Hagendorff's (2020) categorization of AI ethics. "Supportive attitudes," "Power issues" and "Technical solutions" are three themes that are intertwined with Hagendorff's work, while "Vulnerable Groups" and "Capitalism" rely on other research on AI and economy (Fountain, 2021; Piketty, 2020; Tiyasha et al., 2020; Xiang et al., 2021). We provided all themes and subthemes utilized during the analysis (see Table 1.2), which focused on the interpretative level to understand the themes' universal connotations and implications concerning contemporary research on AI ethics (Hagendorff, 2020; Patton, 1990). We note that "Vulnerable groups" should fall under "Supportive attitudes" but methods-wise, our separation relies on the features of "Supportive attitudes" based on former ethical guidelines that mostly lack marginalized circles (Hagendorff, 2020). Therefore, we created a unique category for vulnerable entities.

We chose paragraphs as coding units to avoid thematic discontinuities (Rooduijn, 2014). We coded every theme within the specific paragraph where topics were perceived. The structure of the themes is as follows: we created five themes and thirteen subthemes. We marked themes with numbers ranging between 1 and 5 and utilized letters with small captions to introduce subthemes (see Tables 1.2–1.4). The rest of this section briefly introduces our categories to characterize the typology that helped us conduct the thematic content analysis.

We aimed to understand how the visions and goals of the HAI approaches relate to the increasing inequalities of capitalism (Piketty, 2020) in the published content of these university departments. We believe that such educational institutions should strive to analyze the topics below, elaborate on possible solutions and redress the grievances that harm people globally.

Capitalism: the universal system that prioritizes "the endless accumulation of capital" (Wallerstein, 2004, p. 24), sustains or deepens crises for specific societies or communities, especially in the Global South (Böröcz, 2009; Piketty, 2014, 2020). We aim to understand how the human-centered approach

Table 1.2 Structure and frequencies of themes and subthemes

Themes	*Frequency*
1. Capitalism	*16*
2. Vulnerable groups	*420*
3. Power issues (decision-making)	*673*
4. Supportive attitudes	*1,704*
a. Social responsibility and sustainability	206
b. Welfare	180
c. Help	488
d. Care and nurture	830
5. Technical solutions	*1,049*
e. Safety	223
f. Robustness	44
g. Explainability	29
h. Accountability	48
i. Privacy	161
j. Responsibility	95
k. Non-maleficence (causing no harm)	48
l. Justice and fairness	344
m. Transparency	57
Total	3,862

Table 1.3 Crosstab with themes, column percentages based on the number of documents in which themes appear (row "N = documents")

	University of Bologna	*Utrecht University*	*University of Maryland*	*Northwestern University*	*Stanford University*
1. Capitalism	0	0	0	0	2.8%
2. Vulnerable groups	3.1%	16.9%	9.6%	25.0%	34.1%
3. Power issues (decision-making)	6.3%	27.1%	7.4%	13.9%	48%
4. Supportive attitudes	34.4%	42.4%	23.4%	27.8%	72.2%
5. Technical solutions	12.5%	39%	14.9%	16.7%	58%

relates to capital accumulation and vital wealth inequalities emerging at sub- and supranational levels.

Vulnerable groups: it refers to any group harmed by racism, sexism, gender bias, xenophobia, nativism, antisemitism, islamophobia, economic crises or environmental crises. Marginalized groups such as the Global South, LGBTQ communities, religious and ethnic minorities, refugees, immigrants, low-income citizens and people with physical or cognitive disabilities also belong to these circles (Fountain, 2021). The theme also includes the direct juxtaposition of the elite's interests versus the exposed ones.

Power issues (decision-making): making decisions over people's lives without asking their opinion about the implemented policies by governments or tech corporations. The theme entails decision-makers' activities, including controlling AI by measures or abusing power by surveillance techniques based on AI-driven technology, such as the Chinese "scoring system" (Starke & Lünich, 2020).

Supportive attitudes: according to Hagendorff's (2020) argument, these subthemes do not emerge remarkably in the "Technical solutions" category within AI ethics:

a. Social responsibility: policies that address societal challenges, public engagement activities, charitable giving and efforts to benefit a sustainable environment.
b. Welfare: this subtheme is not axiomatic as it deals with a severe dichotomy; thus, we analyzed whether (1) the connection of AI and welfare refers to sustaining (welfare's) status quo and disregarding policies on decreasing inequalities or (2) it analyzes how AI could ease major wage and redistribution cleavages between classes and regions.

Table 1.4 Crosstab with themes and subthemes, column percentages based on the number of documents in which themes and subthemes appear

	University of Bologna	*Utrecht University*	*University of Maryland*	*Northwestern University*	*Stanford University*
1. Capitalism	0	0	0	0	2.8%
2. Vulnerable groups	3.1%	16.9%	9.6%	25.0%	34.1%
3. Power issues (decision-making)	6.3%	27.1%	7.4%	13.9%	48.0%
4. Supportive attitudes	–	–	–	–	–
a. Social responsibility and sustainability	28.1%	30.5%	2.1%	19.4%	23.3%
b. Welfare	0	1.7%	1.1%	2.8%	25.6%
c. Help	0	1.7%	14.9%	2.8%	48.3%
d. Care and nurture	9.4%	22.0%	10.6%	11.1%	49.4%
5. Technical solutions	–	–	–	–	–
e. Safety	6.3%	23.7%	10.6%	8.3%	27.3%
f. Robustness	0	1.7%	2.1%	0	8.5%
g. Explainability	3.1%	8.5%	1.1%	2.8%	3.4%
h. Accountability	3.1%	1.7%	0	0	8.5%
i. Privacy	3.1%	6.8%	10.6%	0	18.5%
j. Responsibility	0	5.1%	1.1%	0	11.6%
k. Non-maleficence (causing no harm)	0	3.4%	0	5.6%	7.7%
l. Justice and fairness	6.3%	18.6%	2.1%	8.3%	33.2%
m. Transparency	3.1%	11.9%	0	0	9.4%

c. Help: this subtheme includes any effort aiding marginalized communities, people in need or fighting against climate change.
d. Care and nurture: any activity related to healthcare or arguments on necessary equipment and innovations in medical treatment; taking care of young children to keep their systems developing and healthy.

Technical solutions: Hagendorff's argument is based on Gilligan's claims (1982), that is, male-dominated justice ethics are calculating, rational and logic-oriented, mostly disregarding the ethics of empathic and emotion-oriented care:

e. Safety: avoiding AI "side-effects," such as harmful multi-agent approaches, uncertainty, hacking and accidents in machine-learning systems, are parts of this subtheme (Amodei et al., 2016).

f. Robustness: building reliable and secured machine-learning systems is a crucial area of AI studies.
g. Explainability: this subcategory implies arguments on how and why an artificial intelligence algorithm makes decisions while preserving its accuracy.
h. Accountability: it is a closely related concept to transparency, which needs transparent processing operations. In short, accountability can be considered as vital data protection and privacy emphasizing principle (Vedder & Naudts, 2017).
i. Privacy: machine-learning capabilities can put privacy and data protection at risk. Consequently, any text unit that argues the issue of privacy is relevant to this theme.
j. Responsibility: one of the essential questions in AI techniques and machine-learning capabilities considers the entity which is responsible for (1) programming the algorithm, (2) controlling its functions and (3) taking responsibility for harmful happenings, for instance, accidents, caused by AI-driven programs.
k. Non-maleficence: causing no harm should be vital for planning and operating AI-driven technologies. This theme falls under analyzing possible harmful physical and psychological effects and preventing measures.
l. Justice and fairness: on the one hand, AI-driven technology should be controlled by law and order to rightfully involve the court of justice if any non-compliant activity is perceived. On the other hand, unfairness might refer to the fact that AI-based calculations obstruct several marginalized groups from receiving loans and medical care, distracting the opportunity to provide fair services by avoiding gender, race and financial bias.
m. Transparency: it is an essential element of efficient accountability frameworks by ensuring that an algorithmic process is observable and information considering future behavior is supplied (Alhadeff et al., 2012).

Results and Analysis

How the Institutes Define HAI

First, we provide the descriptions of the institutes' definitions of human-centered artificial intelligence to overview their approaches in this research area and seek possible connections between the visions.

The Utrecht University mostly stresses personalization; therefore, it describes HAI as a developing technique that understands and predicts human choice behavior and convinces people to make efficient and environment-friendly decisions, including intelligent interactive information systems and personalized interaction to maximize user satisfaction. This interpretation regards HAI as a product that is designed to be sold and foster convenience.

The University of Maryland imagines a possible, alternative future filled with devices that dramatically amplify human abilities, empower people and ensure human control. This institution considers HAI a tool designed for the people but avoids mentioning business interests and gaining profit. According to the institute's vision, HAI enables people to perceive, create, think and act by combining user experiences with embedded AI support services that users desire.

Stanford University claims that HAI develops frameworks representing different stakeholders, focusing on interdisciplinary collaboration in AI design, development and management. Stanford University's explicit vision for HAI is to develop a tool that fosters a better future for humanity.[2] Therefore, the research institute argues that AI's design team must comprise humanity's broad representatives. It claims that the creators of AI have a collective responsibility to guide machine-learning approaches in an ethical way, that is, fostering positive effects on the globe. This research institute declares that it aims to help future leaders prepare to "learn, build, invent and scale with purpose, intention and a human-centered approach."[3] On the contrary, the broad access of ordinary people to AI techniques is missing from the statement above because it focuses on an AI designing process aligned with "optimistic techno-scientific visions" (Dandurand et al., 2020, p. 600).

Northwestern University defines HAI as a socio-technical system to advance decision-making and "creative and analytical thinking, feeling, and doing." The institute's introduction highlights that machine-learning and data-mining approaches are to augment "human emotion, cognition, and behavior."

The University of Bologna emphasizes that machine-learning approaches are helpful in the fight against organized crime, cyberbullying, cybercrimes, fake news and hate speech. The Italian university claims that HAI techniques are necessary to resist criminal activities. In other words, the University of Bologna defines HAI as a sufficient tool to fight against these phenomena. In contrast, the University of Bologna does not define how AI-driven techniques could prevent the proliferation of the challenges above.

In a nutshell, every institution has a unique approach to HAI but lacks universal values except one: they define HAI in relation to the people. These departments primarily suggest that HAI, in some ways, is adjusted to people's needs. This is an important finding because the departments above suggest, in a very diverging way, though, that HAI is mainly for all of humankind and not for profit accumulation (Wallerstein, 2004). Although it is important to mention that Utrecht University, to a certain extent, tends to consider AI as a product. Critically, however, these definitions have vital limitations. For example, the definitions treat humanity as a homogenous mass, sharing universal goals, needs and interests. Even though people are born with equal dignity and have the right to happiness, we argue that humanity is not homogenous: diverging people and regions struggle mostly with different and sometimes overlapping challenges. Therefore, we argue that AI and ethics attached to the design process can be humanistic if adjusted sensitively to "individual" situations (Hagendorff, 2020). In addition, as we will show later, the institutes often highlight challenges for the local marginalized communities but mostly disregard problems proliferating in the Global South, such as the lack of water supply, starvation, diseases and wars that affect a significant part of Africa and a large part of Asia and South America.

General Outcomes

We introduce our in-depth analysis with specific examples to give insights into our main arguments, starting with the relation between capitalism and the visions of AI. Even though our analysis is qualitative, we aim to present the detailed findings of the theme proportions, which help us compare the institutions' agenda setting on the HAI imaginary and its bonds to the topics above (see Tables 1.2–1.4).

We coded numerous paragraphs (n = 3,862) and perceived that the most frequent theme is Supportive attitudes (n = 1,704) followed by Technical solutions (n = 1,049), Power issues (n = 673), Vulnerable groups (n = 420) and Capitalism (n = 16).[4] Table 1.3 presents the aggregated results of themes and subthemes and suggests that the Supportive attitudes category is the most frequently emerging theme in every institute's published content. Stanford University publishes the most content, as it provides almost four times more texts than the second-most "productive" college, namely the University of Maryland. Additionally, Stanford University produces more content than the other institutions together. Stanford University covers every theme and subtheme, while the University of Bologna is the least diverse in terms of themes. The most productive college dominates every theme and most of the subthemes with three exceptions: Social responsibility and sustainability emerge with larger shares on the two European universities' websites, and Explainability and Transparency occur with a higher share in Utrecht University's online content than on Stanford University's webpage (see Table 1.4).

An important outcome is that Supportive attitudes emerge more frequently than Technical solutions. In contrast to Hagendorff's (2020) results, which show that the Technical solution theme dominates ethics guidelines, the five analyzed universities rather focus on the Supportive attitudes category than overemphasize the "male-dominated" approach. This outcome suggests that different agenda-setting can be perceived if one contrasts AI ethical guidelines university departments and labs' agendas on HAI.

Specific Analysis

We introduce our findings in detail on the five themes, starting with Capitalism and finishing with Technical solutions. Moreover, we characterize three subthemes from Supportive attitudes: (1) Social responsibility and sustainability, (2) Welfare and (3) Care and nurture because these topics are discussed much more in detail than Help, which is a rather general expression without concrete, programmatic guidelines and suggestions. We scrutinize the three subthemes above because we argue that the COVID-19 pandemic, the ecological crisis and flourishing inequalities are intertwined and should be analyzed, if not eased, as soon as possible by the opportunity that artificial intelligence offers us to consider it "human-centered." Note that we do not analyze Technical solutions' subthemes but the theme as a whole because we aim to compare the five main themes to supply an easy-to-follow analysis and focus on the bigger picture to avoid being lost in detail.

Capitalism

A striking result is that only Stanford University considers the theme of capitalism worth mentioning when introducing the visions, goals and expectations for artificial intelligence. The rest of the institutions lack any argument on global capitalism, its ties to artificial intelligence and the institutions' relation to the prevailing economic and political system. In turn, Stanford introduces the pros and cons of capitalism by publishing interviews with persons who support or criticize capital accumulation. A postdoctoral research fellow at Stanford University analyzes the ties between capital accumulation and his institute:

> Stanford certainly has the institutional capital and cultural cachet to influence the AI industry; the question is how it will use that power. The major problems of the 21st century are problems of distribution, not production. There's already enough to go around; the problem is that a small fraction of humanity monopolizes the resources. In this context, making AI more "human-centered" requires focusing on the problems facing the majority of humanity, rather than Silicon Valley.
>
> To pioneer a human-centered AI R&D agenda, thought leaders at Stanford's HAI and elsewhere will have to resist the powerful incentives of global Capitalism and promote things like funding AI research that addresses poor people's problems; encouraging public participation in decision making about what AI is needed and where; advancing AI for the public good, even when it cuts into private profits; educating the public honestly about AI risks; and devising policy that slows the pace of innovation to allow social institutions to better cope with technological change.
>
> (Miller, 2020a)

The argument here has several important implications. First, it stresses that Stanford, with an endowment of more than $15 billion, which places the university among the top four colleges in the United States (Piketty, 2014, p. 447), has enough resources to develop AI-driven techniques that would improve people's well-being globally. Second, it brings attention to a choice that must be made sooner or later from the institute's side: does Stanford develop strategies that might ease global problems or join corporations that chase profit? Finally, the answer above juxtaposes the economic elite with the "common" people and suggests that academics have the role of encouraging the masses to participate in decision-making and informing citizens of AI techniques in detail. Even though the claim above is critical about capitalism, only a few criticisms emerge on Stanford's web page, and most of the content does not touch upon criticism of social and business arrangements for capital accumulation.

Vulnerable Groups

Vulnerable groups appear in every institution's content, but only certain marginalized circles are typically mentioned. Most of the analyzed texts focusing on HAI imaginary related to vulnerable groups considered marginalized circles mostly locally but not globally. This is problematic because the Global South and its vast, struggling masses are underrepresented in the content arguing the visions and goals of HAI.

Considering the ethical questions emerging within the topic of machine-learning algorithms, the University of Utrecht explicitly addresses the problem of biased programming of AI-driven techniques:

> Although computers are often advertised as objective and neutral, the way in which the computers are "raised" provokes questions. Doubts arise on whether or not the current anti-discrimination laws are well-equipped enough to deal with this and if they provide the necessary safeguards.
>
> (University of Utrecht, 2019)

The Dutch university suggests that artificial intelligence is far from neutral because it is created by humans who may have stereotypes, be pressured in design processes, lack empathy, or not care about the potential adverse impact of AI on marginalized groups. Sadly, the analyzed contents do not explain how vulnerable groups should be defended from biases.

Stanford University has the highest percentage of texts of all the institutions dealing with vulnerable groups. In turn, it acknowledges that the research field of AI and academia generally has not yet reflected diversity issues to the necessary extent, and it will take time to change such systemic problems. Even though Stanford University deals the most with vulnerable groups, it is important to emphasize that it mainly mentions vulnerable groups living within the United States but rarely highlights other marginalized groups' problems and the possible solutions, such as ceasing starvation, poverty and life-threatening jobs for the majority residing in the Global South. The example below shows an essential but local problem, which is Hispanic people's, black communities', and women's underrepresentation in American history textbooks used in Texas:

> The most dramatic finding in the Texas history project was the virtual absence of Hispanic people, who received almost no attention outside of the Mexican-American War. Women fared better, but they too were discussed far less frequently than men.
>
> (Andrews, 2020)

The HAI institutes' web pages mainly concentrate on the Global North and its challenges in an era when AI "should be built so as to have net benefits for the whole of society" (Baum, 2017, p. 544) that could contribute to bettering the lives of poorer societies, such as beneficence, non-maleficence, autonomy, justice, explicability, safety and early disease detection (Berberich et al., 2020; Floridi & Cowls, 2021). Among others, we argue that water supply is a key segment of redressing vulnerable groups' grievances, especially in the Global South. The sufficient supply of drinking water by AI is a vital opportunity to support the survival of the most vulnerable ones and prevent several fatal or non-fatal diseases. Artificial intelligence's role in supporting sufficient water supply implies repairing eroded equipment, analyzing water quality and detecting inhabited areas without drinking water. Stanford University mentions problems with water supply in the Global South, however, only to a minimal degree. For example, there are instances where it is discussed that satellites and AI techniques might augment each other and foster mapping of African countries' poor infrastructure. Consequently, constructing water-supplying pipelines could be developed much more precisely due to the rich data analyzed by AI-driven software.

Power Issues

The theme of Power issues has close ties to legislation and measures on artificial intelligence decision-making. Every institute published content on power issues, but on a very different scale: the University of Bologna focused on the smallest, while Stanford University on the largest extent on this theme.

Interestingly, large tech companies' power, that is, collecting, sharing, or exploiting user data for commercial or political goals, emerges to a different extent in the analyzed institutes' content. Even though the University of Bologna's education program implements the intersection of AI and business, we did not find any evidence of criticizing big tech's power supported by AI on the institute's website.

Texts published via Stanford University's HAI website have different approaches to power issues and large tech corporations, with mainly a common aspect: accountability. Some of these articles argued that laws initiated by the US government must regulate big tech companies; others suggested that companies should regulate themselves. Cathy O'Neill, the author of Weapons of Math Destructions, argued in an interview conducted at Stanford University that three diverging aspects could be perceived as related to power imbalance and accountability, namely in the (1) United Kingdom and "Europe," (2) China and (3) the United States. In particular, the following argument reflects on facial recognition systems' unethical coded bias:

> [I]n the States, we live in the wild, wild west. We are home to these tech companies and yet don't have meaningful regulations. Arguably there are more laws that govern my behavior as an independent filmmaker trying to get broadcast on PBS than govern Facebook where a billion people go for their information and political speech.
>
> (Miller, 2020b)

The interviewee suggests that the United States' federal government should regulate facial recognition software by law, and these measures must rely on transparent guidelines to balance big tech's power, which creates these surveillance programs to avoid prejudice.

The Utrecht University joins the argument by emphasizing the role of ethical designing in responsible, autonomous systems:

> Increasingly, computer systems with some degree of autonomy are being employed in practice. Such artificially intelligent software can do things that, when done by humans, are regulated by law. For example, self-driving cars have to obey the traffic laws, online information systems have to comply with data protection law, care robots can damage property or the health of the persons they care for, and autonomous weapons have to comply with the laws of war.
>
> (University of Utrecht, 2021)

Even though GDPR-regulations started within the EU and the United Kingdom, the Utrecht University goes further and elaborates on guidelines for governments—they did not outline which governments they refer to—that should use mobile phone data to design effective measures during the proliferating pandemic. Privacy concerns, however, arise and the institution suggests that data anonymization could protect citizens' privacy. Besides the warning above, there is no criticism reflecting upon big tech corporations or any harmful consequences of their AI-driven techniques.

The University of Maryland mostly seeks sponsorships and collaborations with tech companies via its website, but we also perceived content criticizing firms' biases toward women. One of the submitted abstracts of a speaker series argues that big tech companies "create a work environment of bias, hostility and devalue"; therefore, fewer women worked for tech companies in 2014 (25% of the employees) than in 1990 (31%) and females quit rates are also higher than men's deliberative decisions to leave these firms.

Finally, Northwestern University claims that the HAI institute provides "rigorous research insights to industry and government leaders—contributing to future products from international technology companies," but lacks the critical approach to scrutinizing big tech corporations' ties to power issues.

Supportive Attitudes: Social Responsibility and Sustainability, Welfare and Healthcare

We continue our analysis with the theme of Supportive attitudes in which Social responsibility and sustainability is addressed with similar shares except at the University of Maryland, which hardly mentions the issue. Even though Social responsibility and sustainability regularly emerges within the University of Bologna's website, it is not argued how and when AI would contribute to societal questions or ecology-saver policies. Besides, the Italian institute outlines what research on AI should focus on and disregards the implementation of the technique. Utrecht University argues that societal issues and sustainability should be analyzed together because irrigating crops optimally, storing renewable energy and fighting local air pollution are interconnected issues. The vital feature of the argument above is that Utrecht University aims to transform knowledge of the ecosystem by being "open to the outside world." Unfortunately, it did not express when sufficient knowledge would be available and how the recommendations based on these findings should be implemented. Stanford University suggests that the knowledge captured by AI should be translated into "community-based" decision-making processes as soon as possible. According to Stanford University's articles, AI is useful because it can process ecological problems in multiple dimensions, whereas the human brain cannot absorb so much information. In turn, Northwestern University highlights another aspect of societal challenges and social responsibility:

> We face a global demand for new ways of continuously training and reskilling workers, and we need new socio-technical systems to better enable and advance human sensemaking, decision-making, creative and analytical thinking, feeling, and doing. New techniques are needed that integrate artificial intelligence, machine learning and data-mining approaches in the service of augmenting human emotion, cognition, and behavior.
>
> (Northwestern University, 2021)

Northwestern University addresses the problematic issue of the relation between human and non-human labor forces. It suggests that robots and software should be adjusted to fill gaps or ease difficulties for human laborers. Although Northwestern does not argue its recommendations in detail, it collects research papers on the aforementioned challenge (Hong et al., 2020; Zacks & Franconeri, 2020). Professor Susan Athey, an associate director of HAI institute at Stanford University, also brought attention to the role of AI in the labor market: machine-learning approaches should augment more than replace human workers. Additionally, she argues that there are many tools to evaluate data to help displaced workers overcome difficulties if they lose their jobs due to automation. She suggests that finding upskilling courses that suit displaced workers might foster the solution.

The question of welfare barely emerges in four departments' contents. In contrast, Stanford University emphasizes this theme more than others (see Table 1.4). Probably the most exciting argument on welfare and AI is based on the following perception articulated by Sucheta Ghoshal, an assistant professor at the University of Washington who introduces India's case: "It [AI] was presented as supporting a welfare pipeline but ended up being a massive surveillance and security risk used for religious/caste segregation" (Waikar, 2021).

The statement above is important because Ghoshal highlights vital issues. First, her claim refers to Aadhaar, India's large-scale biometric identification system. The argument brings attention to a Global South country that could have benefitted from artificial intelligence but missed the chance to reduce inequality by machine-learning technologies. The biometric identification system, which covers more than 1.2 billion people, was advocated by the Indian government claiming that Aadhaar would reduce fraud and allow the poor to reach more subsidies. Aadhaar, which suffers from several glitches such as network outages, is linked to food subsidies, pensions, medical reimbursements and disaster emergencies. If there is a fault within Aadhaar, which, according to The Guardian's report, regularly emerges, access to subsidies may suddenly stop (Ratcliffe, 2019). Even though surveillance is unethical and can be one of the cornerstones of oppression, we have a different reason to bring attention to the case above. Besides its observatory nature, an error within Aadhaar can be fatal if food subsidies are limited or banned by a bug emerging in the system. In several instances, Aadhaar did not function correctly, and people died due to starvation (Ratcliffe, 2019). We argue that besides surveillance, the fatal consequences of malfunctioning should have been presented in the analyzed documents since famine also poses a threat to the poor, probably in a more serious way than observation. In other words, famine is a more severe problem than observation, but Ghoshal, aligned with "Western" values, emphasizes the latter but does not focus on the former.

Finally, we introduce another essential problem at the intersection of Supportive attitudes and AI ethics: prejudice in healthcare. The most attractive example was provided by Stanford University that considers the role of AI in healthcare as a predicting algorithm, which might suffer from serious prejudice if vulnerable groups' unmet needs for treatment are not resolved:

> For example, a hospital might use its electronic healthcare records to predict which patients are at risk of cardiovascular disease, diabetes or depression and then offer high-risk patients' special attention. But women, Black people, and other ethnic or racial minority groups might have a history of being

> misdiagnosed or untreated for these problems. That means a predictive model trained on historic data could reproduce historical mistreatment or have a much higher error rate for these subgroups than it does for white male patients. (Miller, 2020c)

Stanford University rightfully argues that marginalized groups could keep being mistreated based on AI suggestions—even if the program was created with the best intent—if redistribution remains unfair and the former data is biased.

Technical Solutions

Our results suggest that three subthemes are salient within technical solutions: safety, privacy and justice/fairness. The issues of safety and privacy are regularly intertwined in the analyzed texts, which argue that decision-makers aim to install policies on artificial intelligence and machine-learning algorithms to control big tech companies' endeavors of abusing personal data. However, as Jessica Fjeld argues at Stanford's AI & Human Rights Symposium, the problematic part of governmental regulations is that "offloading of liability onto machines may benefit only the corporations that make those machines, and not society in general." For instance, AI-driven surveillance techniques could be biased, harming mostly Latinos and black communities. Several governments are willing to buy or design these programs and even outline what type of data they aim to collect by surveillance systems. This is the point where justice and fairness kick in. What happens if the program makes false labels and predictions? It will deepen the crisis for societally vulnerable people. The aforementioned problem is aligned with Monaham's argument (2021), in which he claimed that decolonizing surveillance and relevant studies could challenge Western white male supremacy.

Bias in design has emerged as a relevant topic within the AI sphere (Metz, 2021). This is often linked to the fact that technical solutions are still designed mainly by white men. If we look at the web pages of the analyzed institutions, although certain diversity is present—especially in the case of Stanford University—there is still a dominance of white men. Regulation that supports more diverse research teams across the Global South is inevitable if the HAI concept is geared toward creating technical solutions that address grievances rather than maintaining a status quo steeped in racism. Most of the analyzed institutions admit explicitly or implicitly that the current exclusionary nature of technical solutions is unaffordable. In turn, no specific steps have been presented that might challenge the biased-led AI industry.

Conclusion

In this book chapter, we analyzed five research institutes' official web pages having "Human-centered" and "AI" expressions in their names to scrutinize their published content on the HAI approach's visions on humanity and ethical values connected to capitalism, vulnerable groups, power issues, supportive attitudes and technical solutions. Every analyzed research institute is from the Global North, and among many questions, we investigated how they outline the relation of AI-driven techniques to local and global communities. These institutes define the HAI approach differently except for one thing: they outline their definitions related to humankind, which they consider as a homogeneous mass with the same needs. We argue that different groups have diverging needs, but, of course, specific needs, like well-being, can be overlapping.

The five analyzed research institutes bring attention to supportive attitudes rather than technical solutions in their published content. This is an important result because former research highlighted a reversed outcome when ethical guidelines from the non-academic sectors were analyzed (Hagendorff, 2020). In other words, the scrutinized institutes recognize that they should put supportive attitudes at the center of their published content rather than technical documents to demonstrate their humanistic efforts. Stanford University is a salient institute as it published more content than the others and covered every topic we analyzed. Even though Stanford University made the most effort to introduce the visions of HAI ethics, it failed to provide concrete plans for redressing grievances on a global level, resolving surging inequalities in capitalism and fighting against worldwide racism.

Researchers argue that there is a need for constructing bridges between AI ethics and its implementation into technical solutions (Hagendorff, 2020). All institutes acknowledge that they collaborate with tech companies to a certain extent. However, they do not explain how these co-operations will help reduce inequalities, ease starvation, provide water supply, detect the lacking infrastructure and refine biased recognition systems. Detailed, understandable and transparent explanations are crucial to acquire the trust of the public, especially from laborers whose jobs are on the line due to the rapid automatization. We argue that transparent collaborations could foster plans for reducing poverty in the Global North and the Global South because corporations or other organizations could join this effort with their resources and know-how to implement their ethical principles into practice. Until these co-operations are transparent, none of the stakeholders will be motivated to go beyond ethics discourses that operate only as an assurance for the public and investors (Kerr et al., 2020).

The institutes above claim that they collaborate with tech firms and tend not to criticize capitalism or Western neoliberal values (Stark et al., 2021). We found a few paragraphs at Stanford University's HAI website where fair and universal redistribution appears as a pivotal need within capitalist production. We argue that much more content should be published on reducing inequalities. We suggest that the other institutes, along with Stanford University, should make greater efforts together to analyze these challenges and create plans for easing local and global societal challenges. As these institutes are parts of the wealthy countries in the center (Wallerstein, 2004), they have the most extensive resources to help people in need.

One of the ethical values that most institutes emphasize is human responsibility in designing. Some institutes claim that excuses based on the algorithms' neutrality are not defendable because bad designs, mostly affected by poor or the absence of ethics, derive from human errors (Greene et al., 2019). The perspective above is important because it suggests that beyond the aim of ethics-washing in self-regulation (Bietti, 2020), philosophers, social scientists and citizens should be diversely involved in the designing processes. We agree with researchers who argue that building machine-learning systems should be built after profound consultations with citizens with the intention of "understanding of users' characteristics, the methods of coordination, the purposes and effects of an intervention; and with respect for users' right to ignore or modify interventions" (Cowls et al., 2019, p. 19).

As we detected in our analysis, some institutes (primarily Stanford University) introduced that very narrow groups (e.g., engineers) create AI-driven software. Additionally, we found many articles in which the HAI approach appeared concerning local minorities and biases haunting their everyday lives. Why do we emphasize these observations? Extant research proves that tech companies are not motivated to extend their attention beyond these circles and ease the severe challenges of struggling people (Washington & Kuo, 2020). These corporations' main aim is profit accumulation in the center; therefore, they act globally (sell their products anywhere) and think locally (keep profit in the centrum). In turn, HAI research institutes think globally by highlighting their awareness of humanitarian crises beyond the Global North but mostly focusing on local marginalized communities' disadvantages. The Global South and its numerous problems are underrepresented in the ethical and humanistic visions of AI. How can we call it "Human-centered AI" if these problems remain unsolved both in communication and practice? Big tech corporations and institutes from the Global North have the necessary resources and knowledge to utilize ethical practices to redress diverging grievances together in different regions. One of the biggest challenges in such a helpful collaboration is stressed by Stark and colleagues: "how can members of diverse communities, often with asymmetric access to wealth and power, work together to ensure justice, equality, and fairness exist not just in principle but also in practice" (Stark et al., 2021, p. 273). Our findings suggest that the essential question above remains unanswered in detail. Nonetheless, we think that solutions adjusted to the most severe grievances cannot be redressed without implementing struggling communities' will to help in democratic and ethical ways.

Funding

The study was funded by the Hungarian NRDI Office, grant number OTKA K 142207.

Notes

1 For the sake of coherence and simplicity, we refer to departments, institutions, research labs, university units, research areas, etc., utilizing "human-centered" and "AI" in their names as "institutes" or "institutions."
2 The Stanford University's Human-Centered Artificial Intelligence research institute emphasizes its vision on HAI briefly via its title page under the section "Advancing AI research, education, policy, and practice to improve the human condition" (see at https://hai.stanford.edu/) and discusses it in detail under the "About" section (see Welcome to the Stanford Institute for human-centered artificial intelligence—letter from the Denning co-directors. Retrieved January 12, 2022, from https://hai.stanford.edu/about/welcome).
3 See Welcome to the Stanford Institute for human-centered artificial intelligence—letter from the Denning co-directors. Retrieved January 12, 2022, from https://hai.stanford.edu/about/welcome
4 To overview these results, see Table 1.2.

References

Alhadeff, J., Van Alsenoy, B., & Dumortier, J. (2012). The accountability principle in data protection regulation: Origin, development and future directions. In D. Guagnin, L. Hempel, C. Ilten, I. Kroener, D. Neyland, & H. Postigo (Eds.), *Managing privacy through accountability* (pp. 49–82). Palgrave Macmillan. https://doi.org/10.1057/9781137032225_4

Amodei, D., Olah, C., Steinhardt, J., Christiano, P., Schulman, J., & Mané, D. (2016). *Concrete problems in AI safety*. arXiv preprint arXiv:1606.06565. https://www.sciencedirect.com/science/article/pii/S2405896320316013

Andrews, E. L. (2020). *Whose history? AI uncovers who gets attention in high school textbooks*. Retrieved October 5, 2021, from https://hai.stanford.edu/news/whose-history-ai-uncovers-who-gets-attention-high-school-textbooks

Baum, S. D. (2017). On the promotion of safe and socially beneficial artificial intelligence. *AI & Society*, *32*(4), 543–551. https://doi.org/10.1007/s00146-016-0677-0

Beckert, J. (2016). *Imagined futures: Fictional expectations and capitalist dynamics*. Harvard University Press.

Berberich, N., Nishida, T., & Suzuki, S. (2020). Harmonizing artificial intelligence for social good. *Philosophy & Technology*, *33*(4), 613–638. https://doi.org/10.1007/s13347-020-00421-8

Bietti, E. (2020). *From ethics washing to ethics bashing: A view on tech ethics from within moral philosophy*. Proceedings of the 2020 Conference on Fairness, Accountability, and Transparency. https://doi.org/10.1145/3351095.3372860

Böröcz, J. (2009). *The European Union and global social change: A critical geopolitical-economic analysis* (1st ed.). Routledge. https://doi.org/10.4324/9780203873557

Braun, V., & Clarke, V. (2006). Using thematic analysis in psychology. *Qualitative Research in Psychology*, *3*(2), 77–101. https://doi.org/10.1191/1478088706qp063oa

Brown, N., & Rappert, B. (2017). *Contested futures: A sociology of prospective techno-science*. Routledge.

Cowls, J., King, T., Taddeo, M., & Floridi, L. (2019). *Designing AI for social good: Seven essential factors* (SSRN 3388669). https://onwork.edu.au/

bibitem/2019-Cowls,Josh-King,Thomas-etal-Designing+AI+for+Social+Good+Seven+Essential+Factors/

Dandurand, G., Claveau, F., Dubé, J.-F., & Millerand, F. (2020). Social dynamics of expectations and expertise: AI in digital humanitarian innovation. *Engaging Science, Technology, and Society*, *6*, 591–614.

Demeter, M. (2020). *Academic knowledge production and the global South: Questioning inequality and under-representation* (1st ed.). Palgrave Macmillan. https://doi.org/10.1007/978-3-030-52701-3

Dotson, T. (2015). Technological determinism and permissionless innovation as technocratic governing mentalities: psychocultural barriers to the democratization of technology. *Engaging Science, Technology, and Society*, *1*, 98–120.

Floridi, L., & Cowls, J. (2021). A unified framework of five principles for AI in society. In L. Floridi (Ed.), *Ethics, governance, and policies in artificial intelligence* (pp. 5–17). Springer International Publishing. https://doi.org/10.1007/978-3-030-81907-1_2

Fountain, J. E. (2021). The moon, the ghetto and artificial intelligence: Reducing systemic racism in computational algorithms. *Government Information Quarterly*. https://doi.org/10.1016/j.giq.2021.101645

Gilligan, C. (1982). *In a different voice: Psychological theory and women's development*. Harvard University Press.

Greene, D., Hoffmann, A. L., & Stark, L. (2019). *Better, nicer, clearer, fairer: A critical assessment of the movement for ethical artificial intelligence and machine learning*. Proceedings of the 52nd Hawaii International Conference on System Sciences.

Hagendorff, T. (2020). The ethics of AI ethics: An evaluation of guidelines. *Minds and Machines*, *30*(1), 99–120. https://doi.org/10.1007/s11023-020-09517-8

Haraway, D. J. (1991). *Simians, Cyborgs, and Women: The Reinvention of Nature*. New York: Routledge.

Hong, S. R., Hullman, J., & Bertini, E. (2020). Human factors in model interpretability: Industry practices, challenges, and needs. *Proceedings of the ACM on Human-Computer Interaction*, *4*(CSCW1), Article 068. https://doi.org/10.1145/3392878

Kerr, A., Barry, M., & Kelleher, J. D. (2020). Expectations of artificial intelligence and the performativity of ethics: Implications for communication governance. *Big Data & Society*, *7*(1). https://doi.org/10.1177/2053951720915939

Metz, V. (2021). *Who is making sure the AI machines aren't racist?* Retrieved December 19, 2021, from https://www.nytimes.com/2021/03/15/technology/artificial-intelligence-google-bias.html

Miller, K. (2020a). *HAI fellow Colin Garvey: A Zen Buddhist monk's approach to democratizing AI*. Retrieved October 5, 2021, from https://hai.stanford.edu/news/hai-fellow-colin-garvey-zen-buddhist-monks-approach-democratizing-ai

Miller, K. (2020b). *Coded bias: Director Shalini Kantayya on solving facial recognition's serious flaws*. Retrieved October 5, 2021, from https://hai.stanford.edu/news/coded-bias-director-shalini-kantayya-solving-facial-recognitions-serious-flaws

Miller, K. (2020c). *When algorithmic fairness fixes fail: The case for keeping humans in the loop*. Retrieved October 5, 2021, from https://hai.stanford.edu/news/when-algorithmic-fairness-fixes-fail-case-keeping-humans-loop

Monahan, T. (2021). Reckoning with COVID, racial violence, and the perilous pursuit of transparency. *Surveillance & Society*, *19*(1), 1–10.

Northwestern University. (2021). *Human-centered AI*. Retrieved October 5, 2021, from https://hci.northwestern.edu/research/human-centered-ai.html

Patton, M. Q. (1990). *Qualitative evaluation and research methods* (2nd ed.). Sage Publications.

Piketty, T. (2014). *Capital in the twenty-first century*. Belknap Press.

Piketty, T. (2020). *Capital and ideology*. Harvard University Press.

Ratcliffe, R. (2019). *How a glitch in India's biometric welfare system can be lethal*. Retrieved December 19, 2020, from https://www.theguardian.com/technology/2019/oct/16/glitch-india-biometric-welfare-system-starvation

Rooduijn, M. (2014). The mesmerising message: The diffusion of populism in public debates in Western European media. *Political Studies*, *62*(4), 726–744.

Stark, L., Greene, D., & Hoffmann, A. L. (2021). Critical perspectives on governance mechanisms for AI/ML systems. In J. Roberge & M. Castelle (Eds.), *The cultural life of machine learning* (pp. 257–280). Palgrave Macmillan. https://doi.org/10.1007/978-3-030-56286-1_9

Starke, C., & Lünich, M. (2020). Artificial intelligence for political decision-making in the European Union: Effects on citizens' perceptions of input, throughput, and output legitimacy. *Data & Policy*, *2*, Article e16. https://doi.org/10.1017/dap.2020.19

Tiyasha, T., Tung, T. M., & Yaseen, Z. M. (2020). A survey on river water quality modelling using artificial intelligence models: 2000–2020. *Journal of Hydrology*, *585*, 124670. https://doi.org/10.1016/j.jhydrol.2020.124670

University of Utrecht. (2019). *The lunch meeting on algorithms and diversity*. Retrieved October 5, 2021, from www.uu.nl/en/news/the-lunch-meeting-on-algorithms-and-diversity

University of Utrecht. (2021). *AI, ethics and law*. Retrieved October 5, 2021, from www.uu.nl/en/research/human-centered-artificial-intelligence/special-interest-groups/ai-ethics-and-law

Van Lente, H. (2012). Navigating foresight in a sea of expectations: lessons from the sociology of expectations. *Technology Analysis & Strategic Management*, *24*(8), 769–782.

Vedder, A., & Naudts, L. (2017). Accountability for the use of algorithms in a big data environment. *International Review of Law, Computers & Technology*, *31*(2), 206–224. https://doi.org/10.1080/13600869.2017.1298547

Waikar, S. (2021). *Designing anti-racist technologies for a just future*. Retrieved October 5, 2021, from https://hai.stanford.edu/news/designing-anti-racist-technologies-just-future

Wallerstein, I. (2004). *World-system analysis—an introduction*. Duke University Press.

Washington, A. L., & Kuo, R. (2020). *Whose side are ethics codes on? Power, responsibility and the social good*. Proceedings of the 2020 Conference on Fairness, Accountability, and Transparency. https://doi.org/10.1145/3351095.3372844

Xiang, X., Li, Q., Khan, S., & Khalaf, O. I. (2021). Urban water resource management for sustainable environment planning using artificial intelligence techniques. *Environmental Impact Assessment Review*, *86*, 106515. https://doi.org/10.1016/j.eiar.2020.106515

Zacks, J. M., & Franconeri, S. L. (2020). Designing graphs for decision-makers. *Policy Insights from the Behavioral and Brain Sciences*, *7*(1), 52–63. https://doi.org/10.1177/2372732219893712

2 Values, Work and Well-being in Artificial Intelligence Society

Exacerbating Dilemmas in Human Resource Management

Johnny Långstedt and James Arrowsmith

Introduction

There is no doubt that developed economies are undergoing accelerated technological transformation. This is due to incredible technological advances but also societal change, including the ageing workforce and the COVID pandemic which both intensified automation (Acemoglu & Restrepo, 2017; Chauhan, 2021). In this chapter, we discuss the potential cultural consequences of this ongoing transformation for employees, as well as related concerns for the human resource management (HRM) profession, focusing on artificial intelligence (AI) in particular. We draw on Inglehart's (2018) concept of the artificial intelligence society (AIS), which describes the technologically augmented cultural context in which we are likely to find ourselves in the coming years.

The era of radical digital augmentation that began with the exponential growth in computer power, the internet and advanced robotics has prompted conceptualizations that have in common both awe at the possibilities for humankind and fear that digitalization is already driving labour substitution and inequality. Perhaps the most famous of these is the "fourth industrial revolution" or "industrie 4.0" as originally conceived by Klaus Schwab (2016) of the World Economic Forum. Others have referred to "the second machine age" (Brynjolfsson & McAfee, 2014) in similar recognition of epochal scale and implications of technological transformation. How new digital technologies will affect the workforce is highly debated among scholars, who focus on potential impacts on productivity, labor market dynamics and skill requirements.

On the one hand, as these technologies replace repetitive tasks, they effectively help upskill the employment structure through a process of "skill-biased technological change" (Berman et al., 1998). There are also major social gains to be made if productivity gains are shared in the form of higher incomes or reduced working time as well as more meaningful work. Technology is

DOI: 10.4324/9781003299882-2

also driving constant innovation and improvements in the price and quality of products and services provided to consumers. Automation could also help respond to global challenges such as demographic change, which is contributing to labor shortages and increasing the "dependency ratio" in developed countries, as well as climate change by developing the "green economy."

Alternatively, new technologies could make work more structured, intense and impersonal, such as through algorithmic management, and prompt large-scale economic dislocation. This negative view is of a future of work characterized by increased unemployment and job insecurity. It was long ago predicted by Braverman (1974) who forecast the large-scale displacement and proletarianization (de-skilling and casualization) of white-collar and professional work as soon as technologically feasible. Zuboff (1988) similarly observed how early computerization was used to control more than liberate workers from routine tasks. Now, in a turbo-technological era, even *The Economist (2015*) raises alarm at the prospect of "digital Taylorism" and the dehumanization of work. The fear "is less about robots replacing work and more about work being turned into a robot-like experience" (Spencer, 2018, p. 8).

At the same time, automation and AI are expected to replace large numbers of low-skilled workers, including those in white-collar occupations, because machines can now perform routine cognitive tasks, not just manual tasks. One of the more alarmist and high-profile studies indicated that 47% of US jobs were at risk from automation over the next two decades (Frey & Osborne, 2017). This methodology was criticized for conflating automation of tasks with jobs, but the OECD estimates that one in ten (9%) jobs, especially those of low-qualified workers, are at "serious threat" (Arntz et al., 2016). With rising inequality and precarious employment, including through the growth of platform work, the social security provided by steady work and a welfare state could come to be seen as an historical aberration (Piketty, 2014).

History suggests that technology under capitalism creates more employment than it displaces through a process of "creative destruction" in which new industries, firms and occupations emerge (Schumpeter, 1942; Rumberger, 1984). Certainly, economic history is one of mechanization displacing workers from agrarian to factory to service work, but now that automation threatens routine service work, from retail to the professions, there are concerns about where the replacement jobs will come from, especially as new technology firms hardly employ anyone at all. "Destruction" could come to predominate if machines develop into fully-fledged workers rather than tools that complement human skills (Ford, 2015). Employment would polarize into a small number of knowledge-based roles and fewer lower-skill jobs where requirements for versatility, and low pay, delays automation (OECD, 2016). However, in a rapidly changing world, as the Nobel physicist Niels Bohr pithily observed, "prediction is difficult, especially about the future." The "positive" and "negative" dynamics are likely to unfold simultaneously, with the balance shaped by political choices and interventions as societies respond.

One way in which anticipated work changes impact society is through the challenge they present to their values. According to Inglehart (2018), western democracies were becoming more tolerant and individualistic with each generation after World War II. This was a consequence of improving living standards that promoted "postmaterialist" values, such as concerns with autonomy and self-expression. Psychologically, once people trust that their basic survival needs are met, they can focus resources on discovery; similarly, people are more open to strangers when there are surplus resources, as they are perceived as less of a threat (Inglehart, 2018; Fischer, 2018). As a result, postmaterialist societies tend to be more innovative and tolerant.

Technological transformation jeopardizes this by polarizing skills, work and incomes, especially in neoliberal institutional environments characterized by deregulation and trade union decline. According to Inglehart (2018, p. 207), "Artificial intelligence is hollowing out the economy—replacing secure, well-paid jobs with insecure, poorly paid ones." The AIS accelerates a "winner-takes-all economy," or what Brynjolfsson and McAfee (2014) refer to as a "superstar economy," characterized by extreme economic inequality and a growing class of working poor. For Inglehart (2018), this threatens to unwind postmaterialist values, as indicated by authoritarian and xenophobic political populism in recent years. This is particularly apposite because a recent study shows that those in occupations currently at risk of automation display stronger materialist values than those that are not (Långstedt, 2021a). Because these values become increasingly important in precarious environments, a failure to distribute wealth to the less affluent under AIS threatens to regress societies toward xenophobia and authoritarianism.

At the micro-level of the organization, much of the transformation will be managed by the human resource (HR) function (Halteh et al., 2018). This has specialist responsibilities across the spectrum of employment, including staff recruitment, skills development, labor scheduling, work design, employee relations, reward, performance management and redundancies and redeployment. Artificial intelligence and automation present two sets of challenges for the HR function. The first concerns the inherent tension between acting as an "employee advocate" and a strategic "business partner" (Ulrich & Brockbank, 2005). The former emphasizes the contribution of human capital to business success and focuses on nurturing employee "engagement" through staff involvement, development and meaningful work. The latter means explicitly serving business goals, which are often short-term and cost focused. The use of AI potentially shifts HR toward greater employee surveillance and control and introduces risks such as "algorithmic bias" over recruitment, promotion and other important decisions (Tambe et al., 2019). The second challenge involves the potential hollowing out of the HR function itself as many of its routine activities become automated. Potentially, this frees HR to focus on strategies to better serve its different stakeholders, utilizing data analytics to offer evidence-based proposals, or it could be a recipe for self-redundancy (Charlwood & Guenole, 2022).

In the next section, we focus on the macro-level, exploring how AI could impact societal values through a process of occupational recomposition. Then in the third section we focus on the micro-level of the firm to examine the implications of AI deployment in HRM for the experience of work. The concluding discussion ties together the macro- and organizational perspectives to consider the policy, organizational and HRM ramifications of the changing work landscape.

Values and Well-being in the Artificial Intelligence Society

Work dominates the waking hours of most adults, accounting for roughly a third of their lives between school and retirement. Some argue that without work, our lives become meaningless, while others consider it an obstacle to human growth and thus welcome its substitution (Spencer, 2018). Whichever perspective we adopt, work is central to our being, a source of income and a social context where we contribute our talents and forge bonds with others. Its influence on well-being is well documented in research on unemployment, where a lack of work, and not just income, contributes to poor mental health (van Hal, 2015). A central question in the new socio-economic context brought about by AIS is therefore how it will impact our well-being, to which our values are intimately related (Sagiv et al., 2015). A misalignment between values and work has a negative impact on satisfaction because we prefer to engage in environments where we can attain our values, or at least not have them subverted.

An essential determinant of the impact AI will have on employees is the extent to which the work that it introduces diverges from the human needs that that work originally contributed to. Though specific studies on well-being and AIS are scarce, those that examine the impact of digital technologies at work suggest that they increase worker stress (Ayyagari et al., 2011; Speier & Venkatesh, 2002). This relates to the new competences that employees need to adopt and changes in the work context. Case study research indicates how the alignment of work and values is essential for workers to accept and therefore successfully implement change (Långstedt & Manninen, 2020).

To understand why that is the case, we must consider the characteristics of values. In popular terms, values are the lens through which we observe the world. Of course, values are studied across several disciplines, each with their own methodologies and theories of origins and nature. However, most definitions agree that values represent taken-for-granted guiding principles in life, especially about what is desirable. We adhere to the social scientific perspective represented by, for example, Rokeach (1973), Schwartz (1992) and Inglehart's (1977) theories of values. According to this tradition, values are cognitive representations of basic needs that transcend specific situations and form the basis of our evaluations of the world. Furthermore, and distinct from common personality theories, values have a goal-like nature as they are closely related to our identities and selfhood (Maio, 2015; Maio, 2017; Smith, 1991). We strive to attain our values and achieve a sense of purpose by working toward and aligning our actions with them (Schwartz, 2017).

This strive for purpose is also evident in how values relate to the work, whether in terms of occupational choice (Sagiv, 2002; Knafo & Sagiv, 2004) or experience of job satisfaction, engagement and meaningfulness (Kristof-Brown et al., 2005; Ros et al., 1999). People tend to seek to match their occupation (its tasks, competencies, culture and social contribution) to their values (Holland, 1985; Arieli et al., 2016). This is an essential observation as we move forward to consider how values and well-being relate to AIS, given that values differ across occupations in relation to their susceptibility to automation (Långstedt, 2021a). Furthermore, this difference has been rather stable during the entire 2000's, which demonstrates that little change in European occupational values have occurred and a cultural adaptation to AIS is yet to occur (Långstedt et al. 2023). Based on these findings, and building on prior research on person-job fit, we can suggest that if, in the transition to AIS, available work increasingly requires creative and social tasks, a misalignment between values and work could occur. This could have a depriving impact on well-being for many people, especially at work.

So, let us take a closer look at why AIS might impact well-being negatively, in addition to any negative effect on living standards. In a recent literature review, Sagiv and her colleagues (2015) suggest three complementary ways in which values relate to well-being. One perspective is that some values are inherently healthy. Those positively related to well-being include autonomy, self-expression and a concern for others, and these are more prevalent in non-automatable occupations (Långstedt, 2021). This perspective may become relevant in the long term as "unhealthy" values are more prevalent in precarious and economically deprived contexts. This could trigger a vicious circle, enhancing values that are less fit for success in AIS and having negative consequences for well-being. Another strand of research builds on the goal-like nature of values and stresses the role of value attainment in relation to well-being. The rationale is that the content of values is not directly related to well-being, as in the healthy values perspective, but rather the degree to which values are fulfilled. So, regardless of which values we cherish, we might feel well only if we can attain those values to some extent. Considering the changes that AIS involves, which make life more precarious for many while also placing greater emphasis on autonomy and creativity in jobs, we can expect that attaining values related to conformity and security will become more difficult in AIS.

The third stream of research, and perhaps the most relevant for this discussion, is value congruency, or the "fit" between individual values, needs and interests and the work environment (Maio, 2017). Environments provide certain "affordances" through which we can attain our values. The idea is that work environments (people and tasks) restrict the attainment of some values while supporting the attainment of others. Consider the accounting profession; it provides a structured environment that is highly regulated and predictable. Thus, as an environment, it provides ample opportunities to realize values related to conformity but fewer for the attainment of creativity or autonomy. Another way in which the correspondence between values and the environment affects well-being is through social sanctions and rewards. Social expectations and norms can limit the attainment and expression of deviating values, especially in homogenous contexts. Expressing divergent values is associated with social sanctions and thus relates to poorer well-being. In contrast, expressing convergent values is rewarded and therefore positively impacts well-being. Furthermore, suppressing beliefs that are important to oneself may lead to internal conflicts and consequently poorer well-being.

To understand how well-being could be affected by the changes that AIS involves, we need to consider what values are prevalent in occupations that are most susceptible to automation. The research on this topic is very scarce, and apart from Inglehart's (2018) brief theoretical considerations, we have only identified one empirical study that sheds light on this issue. Långstedt (2021a) used the European Social Survey alongside Frey and Osborne's (2013) analysis of occupational exposure to automation to explore the relationship between values and occupational automatability. This study found that values related to self-transcendence, openness, considering others and autonomy were more prevalent in low-risk occupations and correlated negatively with automation. In contrast, conservation and self-enhancement values, and those relating to stability and self-interest, were more prevalent in susceptible occupations and also correlated positively with automation. If AIS is realized as expected, the latter values "fit" the new requirements poorly as they relate to conformity and stability; furthermore, research has found that they also relate negatively to creativity and social skills that are expected to be crucial for work in AIS (see Långstedt, 2021a, 2021b, or Arieli et al., 2020 for a thorough discussion on values and skills).

These observations are important when considering how well-being is affected by AIS through values. A large share of scholarship on AIS expects routine work to decrease significantly, and this trend has already long been observed in Europe (Goos et al., 2009) and the USA (Autor & Dorn, 2013). If AI replaces routine and, given technological leaps, more complicated but structured work, then jobs that satisfy conservation values will become scarce, or those that remain available will offer increasingly poor compensation and precarity. Whichever the case, a significant challenge is that the values that are least well "fit" for the work requirements in AIS are significantly more prevalent in the occupations that are likely to be replaced by technologies.

Occupations that are characterized by a stronger desire for stability are thus transitioned into a precarious position, or, alternatively, work is in a context that does not support the attainment of these values. Sanctions for pursuing stability and predictability may even be applied because they offer less added value to the employer. It is then quite obvious that the environmental fit perspective becomes relevant in AIS, and this has negative consequences for the well-being of people replaced or otherwise impacted by technologies. They are not able to pursue their values in the work environment and may experience social sanctions if they try.

What Inglehart's (2018) work has shown is that when economic development becomes negative and life becomes more precarious, societies become more materialist, that is, conservative, xenophobic and authoritarian. This is already evident in the voting behavior in deprived contexts in the USA (Inglehart & Norris, 2017). Considering the healthy values perspective, this tendency might become problematic in AIS because materialist values are related to a poorer sense of well-being (Sagiv et al., 2012) and decreased levels of innovation (Purc & Lagun, 2019). This could lead to a vicious circle where AIS actually promotes values that decrease well-being and widen work-value divergences between the values of the poor and the requirements of well-paid jobs. The context that AIS comprises, with its precarity and income inequalities, enhances unhealthy values. It creates a divergence between values and work requirements and inhibits the attainment of the more prevalent values in automatable occupations. Consequently, AIS will broadly decrease well-being.

To summarize, the cultural development of AIS negatively affects the well-being of societies, not only through increased income disparities and precarious lives but also by creating a context that does not support the values of those most likely to be replaced by advanced technologies, and through promoting so-called unhealthy values. For the HRM profession, this involves tensions as the dual role of HR professionals becomes more salient. They are forced to perform a balancing act between their perceived duties to enhance employee well-being—long associated with the professional values and welfarist heritage of the function—and on the other hand, their obligation to serve organizational profitability. In the next section, we take a closer look at the ambiguities, contradictions and ethical considerations arising as the transition to AIS unfolds.

HRM at the Frontline of Work Tensions Arising from Automation

The application of AI in HRM has so far been eclipsed by other business areas such as marketing, which benefit from cleaner and larger datasets (Tambe et al., 2019). These functions also face fewer overt ethical controversies that impede deployment. The intent of marketing may be manipulation, but HR decisions have a potentially huge impact on people's lives, increasing reputational risk (Hamilton & Sodeman, 2020). In addition, most businesses, and HR teams, are too small to embrace advanced technologies (Cappelli, 2017).

Nevertheless, the use of AI systems by HR practitioners has rapidly increased in recent years (Cheng & Hackett, 2021). As the World Economic Forum (2021, p. 5) observes, "developers are creating AI tools for almost every stage of the HR life cycle." The principal HRM applications are threefold:

- recruitment and selection (advertising, screening and interviewing), where the technology is used to analyze textual and visual data.
- algorithmic work management, as exemplified by platform work but also extensively used in regular employment to direct workers (task ordering and labor scheduling), evaluate workers (performance monitoring and rating) and discipline workers through rewards and penalties including dismissal (Kellogg et al., 2020). Amazon is the paradigm case, but these systems are also widely used across the logistics, manufacturing, retail, hospitality and call center sectors. The shift to home-working under COVID also accelerated their deployment across white-collar occupations (EU-OSHA, 2022).
- people analytics, whereby data are analyzed to identify patterns and make predictions to inform decision making around employee engagement, training, turnover intentions and incentives.

In addition, AI systems can be integrated into advanced robotics to enable machines to perform more complex and variable tasks, and enhance the human-machine interface (Fletcher & Webb, 2017).

These AI technologies can be used to support worker wellbeing by improving communication, safety and cooperation and by reducing conflict, bullying and favoritism at work (EU-OSHA, 2022). However, there are growing concerns that "as AI-based algorithms become more widely used, algorithmic HRM is shifting decision-making responsibility from human to machine" (Meijerink et al., 2021, p. 2550). This raises ethical issues around accountability and the potential for embedding and obfuscating bias and discrimination, and there are also concerns around the impact of AI on the number and quality of jobs (Eurofound, 2022).

Bias and Discrimination

Advanced digital technologies can increase the efficiency of recruitment processes and help HRM identify best "fit" candidates. They can also support HR managers to reduce the scope for human prejudice, unconscious bias and unfairness in employment decision making (Deshpande et al., 2021; Thierer et al., 2017). Unfortunately, "while algorithms are often viewed as objective and impartial, they in fact have the potential to encode and amplify existing biases" (WEF, 2021, p. 18). This is because the training data used for machine learning might not be of sufficient scale or representative, based, for example, on white males, and the impact of wider social inequalities—such as access to educational opportunities—are neglected in design (European Parliament, 2020; Loi, 2020). Measures used to appraise employees or job applicants might also be reductive. Recent research indicates that automation of the hiring process imposes narrow and inflexible criteria, to the mutual disadvantage of employers and applicants (Fuller et al., 2021). The result is exclusion and a lack of diversity.

Job Loss

Much of the debate around the impact of automation technologies on employment has been based on modeling rather than empirical research. So far, the evidence indicates that technological change in western countries is net positive in terms of skills, reducing demand for jobs that require fewer qualifications but increasing the numbers employed in skill-intensive work (Oesch & Piccitto, 2019). There is also some recent empirical research based on micro-level data in the United Kingdom (Hunt et al., 2022) and France (Aghion et al., 2019). These studies indicate that the implementation of AI technology simultaneously results in job creation and job destruction. The automation of some tasks may mean fewer people are needed to perform some jobs, but increased productivity may reduce costs, therefore stimulating sales and demand for workers overall. The overall effect is positive, notwithstanding job losses at non-automating competing firms, but less educated workers are more adversely impacted. This confirms the risk of value incongruence arising from AIS discussed in the previous section.

This process might unfold because lower-skilled workers are seen as more of a cost than an investment. As Andrew Puzder, the former CEO of Carl's Jr and President Trump's nominee for Labor Secretary, observed,

> if you're making labor more expensive, and automation less expensive, this is not rocket science. Machines are always polite, they always upsell, they never take a vacation, they never show up late, there's never a slip-and-fall, or an age, sex or race discrimination case.

Hiring a person means wages, taxes, insurance and other costs as well as potential problems and disputes; hiring a machine is tax-deductible capital expenditure. COVID is expected to accelerate the automation of these jobs, both in response to labor shortages and to safeguard against future pandemics (Chernoff & Warman, 2020), as well as make inroads into higher-skill work as the pandemic served to increase the profile and reduce the cost of "Intelligent Automation" processes (Coombs, 2020). All of which increases the pressure on HR to manage redundancies, retraining and redeployment of staff.

Job Quality

The implications of AI and automation for the experience of work are an important and much-discussed but less well-researched issue. Qualitative research indicates that the application of AI can enhance job flexibility, autonomy and creativity for employees, but this does not make up for the "technostress" experienced as a result of coping with change (including job losses) and the heightened complexity, accountability, urgency and work overload that results (Malik et al., 2022). In some circumstances, automation can make jobs more structured and limited (Smids et al., 2020; Andersson et al., 2022), as well as promote job insecurity and inferior terms and conditions through outsourcing (De Stefano, 2018; Berg, 2019). Algorithmic scheduling can lead to casualization, especially in regions where jobs are scarce and workers are less able to resist (Gilbert & Thomas, 2021).

Workers can also be distressed by increased monitoring and surveillance (Ball, 2021). Integrated technologies offer employers a seductive panoply of techniques to better monitor and intensify work, including keystroke logging, computer and internet recording and tracking worker movements. The lack of transparency around the collection, processing and use of large volumes of employee data results in employees having an informational disadvantage, leading to anxiety and hyper-conformity (Dagnino & Armaroli, 2019). From an ethical point of view, this is dangerous because "algorithm-based HR decisions may harm employees' personal integrity," intensifying control by impersonal means (Leicht-Deobald et al., 2019). Conceivably, the "datafication of work" could also make workers reluctant to exercise their employment rights because of the risk to their "online reputation" and future job prospects (Todolí-Signes, 2021).

Running across each of these three sets of risks is the reinforcement of disadvantage by gender, age, race and disability. To take gender as an example, AI is transforming the labor market in multiple gendered ways (European Institute for Gender Equality, 2021). Women are more likely to work in occupations that involve a high degree of routine and repetitive tasks (e.g., clerical support work or retail jobs), so they are at greater risk of job loss through automation and are under-represented in growth occupations such as information technologies. As noted, AI can reinforce discriminatory hiring practices and other decision making due by embedding bias into its design. Finally, with more people working from home due to the COVID-19 pandemic, the use of algorithmic monitoring and surveillance tools has increased to track workers' activity in real time. However, these have potentially discriminatory effects as female remote workers are more likely to have to attend to children or other family members, which impacts on these performance metrics.

As argued earlier, the challenges posed by AI applications in HR—potential discrimination, job loss and deteriorating job quality—imply immense upheaval, including through the threat to established occupational and social values. At the micro-level, much depends on context, including organizational size and sector; occupational labor market conditions, notably worker skill and scarcity value; and trade union organization and state regulation. In line with Socio-Technical Systems and Varieties of Capitalism theories, the process and effects of automation may be more benign in "coordinated market economies" (CMEs) than in "liberal market economies" (LMEs) owing to greater provision for worker involvement and a bias toward functional (skills-based) flexibility rather than numerical flexibility within deregulated labor markets (Hall & Soskice, 2001). The implications for the activities and values of the HR function itself will also similarly vary, with greater opportunity to serve both employees and the business in those organizations, sectors and national business systems that are geared toward competition on the basis of quality and innovation rather than simply cost (Schuler & Jackson, 1987).

Discussion

The effects of technologies such as AI in the workplace are not deterministic but shaped by social context including organizational goals that, in turn, tend to represent prevalent social norms. On the one hand, technology offers a means of surveillance and oppression, but on the other, it could help management make decisions to improve employee well-being by monitoring stress and reorganizing work. By substituting for labor intensive but low value adding or dull work, artificial intelligence and other advanced technologies can help companies overcome potential labor shortages caused by demographic change or the effects of COVID, as well as make work more interesting for employees.

Precarity and changing work requirements are the essential mechanisms through which values affect well-being in AIS. We identified three phenomena that are highly relevant for HRM and through which advanced technologies can reconstruct work, making working-life more precarious and adversely impacting well-being: bias and discrimination, job loss and decreased job quality. The risk is that a poorly managed AI process exaggerates rather than mitigates work-value incongruence. To minimize harm and maximize mutual gains, HR needs to closely involve employees in the design, implementation, monitoring and review of AI tools that impact them and their work (WEF, 2021). Leading this process can also enhance the status and business credibility of the HR function itself.

Advanced technologies clearly have the potential to cater both to the "human" and "resources" foci of HRM. The tension between employee well-being and the business side of HRM, however, will become sharper in AIS as companies substitute workers to realize productivity gains. The recomposition of employment that AIS introduces is particularly relevant regarding the meaningfulness of work, and thereby employee well-being. Because values in automatable occupations are more inclined toward materialism, and because these values are negatively related to the majority of skills required to prosper in AIS (Långstedt, 2021a), the favoring of creative work is challenging to a large share of the population. These challenges are likely to be accentuated by the work context if employment relations become more precarious and we enter an era of gig work and inequality, because materialist values become more important in such contexts (Inglehart, 2018). This could make populations less innovative to the detriment of the individuals and businesses in AIS.

The relationship between values and well-being poses several different challenges for HRM. First, how can the function promote so-called healthy values when the societal context in AIS is rigged to do the opposite? According to the Resource-Based View of the firm, organizational culture, knowledge and employee competencies offer a unique and sustainable source of competitive advantage that HR can manage and deploy (Whitfield, 2019). Shaping organizational environments and employment relationships to enhance innovation and creativity in this way includes measures to enhance job security, worker involvement and upskilling, which can also nudge values in a healthier direction.

The second challenge for values and well-being in AIS is that attaining "materialist values," for example, security, becomes increasingly difficult or unlikely. Again, central to this issue is the observation that people in automatable occupations tend to emphasize materialist values, which become less attainable in a precarious environment. A central question for HRM in AIS is to consider, on the one hand, how to support employees in attaining their values to increase engagement and well-being, and, on the other hand, ensure the productivity and innovation of the personnel. The controversy of the situation is that as businesses and working life in AIS rely increasingly on innovation and social skills, how will future HR managers enable the attainment of materialist values in a context that requires the opposite of structure, conformity and predictability? It could be that values shift to better align with the new realities, but in the meantime, rewards and incentives could be offered to reconcile materialist values with innovation. Such solutions would mitigate the negative impacts of diverging work values fit on well-being and engagement in AIS.

Finally, with regard to the values-environment fit, the challenge is a societal one in which AIS reduces social mobility and exacerbates and solidifies class differences. This is because materialist values do not provide a strong basis for innovation, leading to social sanctions in the form of lower pay and fewer employment opportunities for those holding such values, so negatively impacting well-being. The risk is that well-being becomes a prerogative limited to the affluent echelons of society. To mitigate this, society needs to enhance education, and the HR function connects to this through better vocational training and lifelong learning.

The professional self-perception of HRM is that it serves the business but does this by being responsible in its treatment of employees. Employees have different values, but these tend to cluster around certain occupations. In AIS, it is hardly justified from a business perspective to reward actions that contradict innovation, but employee well-being for those that cherish materialist values is tied to conformist and risk-avoiding behavior. One way around this is for the HRM function to help shape an organizational environment where a diversity of values is considered legitimate. Rudimentary attempts to develop frameworks for managing value diversity exist (e.g., Långstedt et al., 2017), but regretfully, this field of research currently lacks a practical research agenda (Långstedt, 2021b). One priority for HR managers would be to screen applicants for leadership positions so that "soft skills" and inclusive values are emphasized at least as much as technical abilities in the management role.

In conclusion, the transformation of working life, the adoption of technologies and their use involve social rather than technical decisions. Technologies do not require managers to monitor workers; rather, the desire of managers to do so creates a demand for such technologies. In organizations, the HRM function has a key role in defining how technologies are used, including whether they enhance or degrade working lives. From a wider social perspective, job loss does not necessarily lead to existential insecurity if social security policies and retraining opportunities are in place to soften the blow. Indeed, based on the current understanding of values and the literature discussed above, social security would promote an *artificial intelligence society* characterized by innovativeness, inclusivity and well-being rather than uninventiveness and malaise. In the words of Mahatma Gandhi, "The future depends on what we do in the present." It is crucial that the HR profession as well as policy makers at higher levels start planning for the future now.

References

Acemoglu, D., & Restrepo, P. (2017). Secular stagnation? The effect of aging on economic growth in the age of automation. *American Economic Review: Papers & Proceedings*, 174–179.

Aghion, P., Antonin, C., & Bunel, S. (2019). Artificial intelligence, growth and employment: The role of policy. *Economie et Statistique/Economics and Statistics*, *510*(1), 149–164. https://doi.org/10.24187/ecostat.2019.510t.1994

Andersson, C., Hallin, A., & Ivory, C. (2022). Unpacking the digitalisation of public services: Configuring work during automation in local government. *Government Information Quarterly*, *39*(1), 101662. https://doi.org/10.1016/j.giq.2021.101662

Arieli, S., Sagiv, L., & Cohen-Shalem, E. (2016). Values in business schools: The role of self-selection and socialization. *Academy of Management Learning and Education*, *15*(3), 493–507. https://doi.org/10.5465/amle.2014.0064

Arieli, S., Sagiv, L., & Roccas, S. (2020). Values at work: The impact of personal values in organisations. *Applied Psychology*, *69*(2), 230–275. https://doi.org/10.1111/apps.12181

Arntz, M. U., Gregory, T., & Zierahn, U. (2016). *The risk of automation for jobs in OECD countries: A comparative analysis* (OECD Social, Employment and Migration Working Papers No. 189). OECD. https://doi.org/10.1787/5jlz9h56dvq7-en

Autor, D. H., & Dorn, D. (2013). The growth of low-skill service jobs and the polarization of the US labor market. *American Economic Review, 103*(5), 1553–1597. https://doi.org/10.1257/aer.103.5.1553

Ayyagari, R., Grover, V., & Purvis, R. (2011). Technostress: Technological antecedents and implications. *MIS Quarterly: Management Information Systems, 35*(4), 831–858. https://doi.org/10.1017/CBO9781107415324.004

Ball, K. (2021). *Electronic monitoring and surveillance in the workplace: Literature review and policy recommendations*. Publications Office of the European Union, Luxembourg.

Berg, J. (2019, May 31). *Protecting workers in the digital age: Technology, outsourcing and the growing precariousness of work.* SSRN. https://papers.ssrn.com/sol3/Delivery.cfm/SSRN_ID3413740_code690094.pdf?abstractid=3413740

Berman, E., Bound, J., & Machin, S. (1998). Implications of skill-biased technological change: International evidence. *Quarterly Journal of Economics, 113*(4), 1245–1279.

Braverman, H. (1974). *Labor and monopoly capital: The degradation of work in the twentieth century*. Monthly Review Press.

Brynjolfsson, E., & McAfee, A. (2014). *The second machine age: Work, progress and brilliant technologies*. W. W. Norton & Company Inc.

Cappelli, P. (2017, June). There's no such thing as big data in HR. *Harvard Business Review*.

Charlwood, A., & Guenole, N. (2022). Can HR adapt to the paradoxes of artificial intelligence? *Human Resource Management Journal*. https://doi.org/10.1111/1748-8583.1243

Chauhan, A. (2021). Robotics and Automation: The Rescuers of COVID Era. In: Oliva, D., Hassan, S.A., Mohamed, A. (Eds.), Artificial Intelligence for COVID-19. *Studies in Systems, Decision and Control*, vol 358. Springer, Cham. https://doi.org/10.1007/978-3-030-69744-0_8

Cheng, M. M., & Hackett, R. D. (2021). A critical review of algorithms in HRM: Definition, theory, and practice. *Human Resource Management Review, 31*(1). https://doi.org/10.1016/j.hrmr.2019.100698

Chernoff, A. W., & Warman, C. (2020, November). *COVID-19 and implications for automation* (NBER Working Paper No. 27249). NBER. https://doi.org/10.3386/w27249

Coombs, C. (2020). Will COVID-19 be the tipping point for the intelligent automation of work? A review of the debate and implications for research. *International Journal of Information Management, 55*. https://doi.org/10.1016/j.ijinfomgt.2020.102182

Dagnino, E., & Armaroli, I. (2019). A seat at the table: Negotiating data processing in the workplace—a national case study and comparative insights. *Comparative Labor Law and Policy Journal, 41*(1), 173–195.

Deshpande, A., Picken, N., Kunertova, L., De Silva, A., Lanfredi, G., & Hofman, J. (2021). *Improving working conditions using artificial intelligence*. Policy Department for Economic, Scientific and Quality of Life Policies, European Parliament.

De Stefano, V. (2018). *"Negotiating the algorithm": Automation, artificial intelligence and labour protection*. International Labour Organization.

The Economist. (2015, September 10). Digital Taylorism. *The Economist*.

Eurofound. (2022). *Ethics in the digital workplace*. Publications Office of the European Union. https://doi.org/10.2806/641341

European Agency for Safety and Health at Work (EU-OSHA). (2022). *Artificial intelligence for worker management: An overview*. Publications Office of the European Union.

European Institute for Gender Equality. (2021). *Artificial intelligence, platform work and gender equality*. Publications Office of the European Union.

European Parliament. (2020). *The ethics of artificial intelligence: Issues and initiatives*. European Parliamentary Research Service.

Fischer, R. (2018). *Personality, values, culture: An evolutionary approach*. Cambridge University Press.

Fletcher, S. R., & Webb, P. (2017). Industrial robot ethics: The challenges of closer human collaboration in future manufacturing systems. In M. I. Aldinhas Ferreira, J. Silva Sequeira, M. O. Tokhi, & E. E. Kadar (Eds.), *A world with robots—international conference on robot ethics: ICRE 2015* (pp. 159–169). Springer.

Ford, M. (2015). *The rise of the robots: Technology and the threat of a jobless future*. Basic Books.

Frey, C. B., & Osborne, M. A. (2013, September). *The future of employment: How susceptible are jobs to computerisation?* (Working Paper). Oxford Martin Programme on Technology and Employment. https://www.oxfordmartin.ox.ac.uk/downloads/academic/future-of-employment.pdf

Frey, C. B., & Osborne, M. A. (2017). The future of employment: How susceptible are jobs to computerisation? *Technological Forecasting and Social Change, 114*, 254–280. https://doi.org/10.1016/j.techfore.2016.08.019

Fuller, J. B., Raman, M., Sage-Gavin, E., & Hines, K. (2021). *Hidden workers: Untapped talent*. Harvard Business School and Accenture.

Gilbert, A., & Thomas, A. (2021). *The Amazonian era: How algorithmic systems are eroding good work*. Institute for the Future of Work.

Goos, M., Manning, A., & Salomons, A. (2009). Job polarization in Europe. *The American Economic Review, 99*(2), 58–63.

Hall, P., & Soskice, D. (2001). An introduction to varieties of capitalism. In P. Hall & D. Soskice (Eds.), *Varieties of capitalism: The institutional foundations of comparative advantage* (pp. 1–70). Oxford University Press.

Halteh, J., Arrowsmith, J., Parker, J., Zorn, T. E., & Bentley, T. (2018). The impact of technology on employment: A research agenda for New Zealand and beyond. *Labour & Industry: A Journal of the Social and Economic Relations of Work, 28*(3), 203–216. https://doi.org/10.1080/10301763.2018.1519774

Hamilton, R. H., & Sodeman, W. A. (2020). The questions we ask: Opportunities and challenges for using big data analytics to strategically manage human capital resources. *Business Horizons, 63*, 85–95.

Holland, L. J. (1985). *Making vocational choices: A theory of vocational personalities and work environments* (2nd ed.). Prentice-Hall.

Hunt, W., Sarkar, S., & Warhurst, C. (2022). Measuring the impact of AI on jobs at the organization level: Lessons from a survey of UK business leaders. *Research Policy, 51*(2). https://doi.org/10.1016/j.respol.2021.104425

Inglehart, R. (1977). *The silent revolution: Changing values and political styles among western publics*. Princeton University Press.

Inglehart, R. (2018). *Cultural evolution: People's motivations are changing, and reshaping the world*. Cambridge University Press.

Inglehart, R., & Norris, P. (2017). Trump and the populist authoritarian parties: The silent revolution in reverse. *Perspectives on Politics, 15*(2), 443–454. https://doi.org/10.1017/S1537592717000111

Kellogg, K., Valentine, M., & Christin, G. (2020). Algorithms at work: The new contested terrain of work. *Academy of Management Annals, 14*(1), 366–410.

Knafo, A., & Sagiv, L. (2004). Values and work environment: Mapping 32 occupations. *European Journal of Psychology of Education, 19*(3), 255–273. https://doi.org/10.1007/BF03173223

Kristof-Brown, A. L., Zimmerman, R. D., & Johnson, E. C. (2005). Consequences of individuals' fit at work: A meta-analysis of Person-Jo. *Personnel Psychology, 58*, 281–342.

Långstedt, J. (2021a). How will our values fit future work? An empirical exploration of basic values and susceptibility to automation. *Labour & Industry: A Journal of the Social and Economic Relations of Work, 31*(2), 129–152. https://doi.org/10.1080/10301763.2021.1886624

Långstedt, J. (2021b). *Towards a model for managing value diversity in the work environment*. Åbo Akademi University. www.doria.fi/handle/10024/180985

Långstedt, J., & Manninen, T. J. (2020). Basic values and change: A mixed methods study. *Journal of Change Management, 21*(3), 333–357. https://doi.org/10.1080/14697017.2020.1837206

Långstedt, J., Wikström, R., & Hellström, M. (2017). Leading human values in complex environments. In J. Vesalainen, K. Valkokari, & M. Hellström (Eds.), *Practices for network management: In search of collaborative advantage* (1st ed., pp. 47–62). Palgrave Macmillan.

Långstedt, J., Spohr, J., & Hellström, M. (2023). Are our values becoming more fit for artificial intelligence society? A longitudinal study of occupational values and occupational susceptibility to technological substitution. Elsevier Enhanced Reader. *Technology in Society, 72*. https://doi.org/10.1016/j.techsoc.2023.102205

Leicht-Deobald, U., Busch, T., Schank, C., Weibel, A, Schaftheitle, S., Wildhaber, I., & Kasper, G. (2019). The challenges of algorithm-based HR decision-making for personal integrity. *Journal of Business Ethics, 160*, 377–392.

Loi, M. (2020). *People analytics must benefit the people: An ethical analysis of data-driven algorithmic systems in human resources management*. AlgorithmWatch.

Maio, G. R. (2017). *The psychology of human values*. Routledge.

Malik, N., Tripathi, S. N., Kar, A. K., & Gupta, S. (2022). Impact of artificial intelligence on employees working in industry 4.0 led organizations. *International Journal of Manpower, 43*(2), 334–354.

Meijerink, J., Boons, M., Keegan, A., & Marler, J. (2021). Algorithmic human resource management: Synthesizing developments and cross-disciplinary insights on digital HRM. *The International Journal of Human Resource Management, 31*(12), 2545–2562.

OECD. (2016). *ICTs and jobs: Complements or substitutes?* (Digital Economy Papers No. 259). OECD.

Oesch, D., & Piccitto, G. (2019). The polarization myth: Occupational upgrading in. *Work and Occupations, 46*(4), 441–469. https://doi.org/10.1177/0730888419860880

Piketty, T. (2014). *Capital in the twenty-first century*. Harvard University Press.

Purc, E., & Lagun, M. (2019, April). Personal values and innovative behavior of employees. *Frontiers in Psychology, 10*. https://doi.org/10.3389/fpsyg.2019.00865

Rokeach, M. (1973). *The Nature of Human Values*. Free Press.

Ros, M., Schwartz, S. H., & Surkiss, S. (1999). Basic individual values, work values, and the meaning of work. *Applied Psychology, 48*(1), 49–71. https://doi.org/10.1080/026999499377664

Rumberger, R. (1984). High technology and job loss. *Technology in Society*, *6*(4), 263–284.

Sagiv, L. (2002). Vocational interests and basic values. *Journal of Career Assessment*, *10*(2), 233–257. https://doi.org/10.1177/1069072702010002007

Sagiv, L., Roccas, S., & Hazan, O. (2012). Value pathways to well-being: Healthy values, valued goal attainment, and environmental congruence. In *Positive psychology in practice* (pp. 68–85). Wiley. https://doi.org/10.1002/9780470939338.ch5

Sagiv, L., Roccas, S., & Oppenheim-Weller, S. (2015). Values and well-being. In *Positive psychology in practice: Promoting human flourishing in work, health, education, and everyday life* (2nd ed., pp. 103–120). Wiley. https://doi.org/10.1002/9781118996874.ch7

Schuler, R., & Jackson, S. (1987). Linking competitive strategies with human resource management practices. *Academy of Management Executive*, *1*, 207–219.

Schumpeter, J. (1942). *Capitalism, socialism, and democracy*. Harper & Bros.

Schwab, K. (2016). *The fourth industrial revolution*. World Economic Forum.

Schwartz, S. H. (1992). Universals in the content and structure of values: Theoretical advances and empirical tests in 20 countries. *Advances in Experimental Social Psychology*, *25*(C), 1–65. https://doi.org/10.1016/S0065-2601(08)60281-6

Schwartz, S. H. (2017). The refined theory of basic values. In S. Roccas & L. Sagiv (Eds.), *Values and behavior: Taking a cross-cultural perspective* (pp. 51–72). Springer.

Smids, J., Nyholm, S., & Berkers, H. (2020). Robots in the workplace: A threat to—or opportunity for—meaningful work? *Philosophy and Technology*, *33*, 503–522.

Smith, M. B. (1991). *Values, self and society toward a humanist social psychology* (2017th ed.). Routledge.

Speier, C., & Venkatesh, V. (2002). The hidden minefields in the adoption of sales force automation technologies. *Journal of Marketing*, *66*(3), 98–111. https://doi.org/10.1509/jmkg.66.3.98.18510

Spencer, D. A. (2018). Fear and hope in an age of mass automation. *New Technology, Work and Employment*, *33*(1), 1–12.

Tambe, P., Cappelli, P., & Yakubovich, V. (2019). Artificial intelligence in human resources management: Challenges and a path forward. *California Management Review*, *61*(4), 15–42.

Thierer, A. D., O'Sullivan, A. C., & Russell, R. (2017). *Artificial intelligence and public policy*. Mercatus Centre, George Mason University.

Todolí-Signes, A. (2021). The evaluation of workers by customers as a method of control and monitoring in firms: Digital reputation and the European Union's general data protection regulation. *International Labour Review*, *160*(1), 65–83.

Ulrich, D., & Brockbank, W. (2005). *The HR value proposition*. Harvard Business School Press.

Van Hal, G. (2015, January 9). The true cost of the economic crisis on psychological well-being: A review. *Psychology Research and Behavior Management*, *8*, 17–25. https://doi.org/10.2147/PRBM.S44732. PMID: 25657601; PMCID: PMC4295900.

Whitfield, K. (2019). The resource-based view approach and HRM. In K. Townsend, K. Cafferkey, A. M. McDermott, & T. Dundon (Eds.), *Elgar introduction to theories of human resources and employment relations* (pp. 324–335). Edward Elgar Publishing.

World Economic Forum. (2021). *Human-centred artificial intelligence for human resources: A toolkit for human resources professionals*. World Economic Forum.

Zuboff, S. (1988). *In the age of the smart machine: The future of work and power*. Basic Books.

3 In the Forefront of Code

Ethics in Decentralized Finance

Andreas Langenohl

Introduction

In her recent proposal of a "cloud ethics," Louise Amoore (2020) suggests that we approach the question of the consequences of ever more complex algorithms on contemporary societies and individual as well as collective agency within them, through a notion of ethics, borrowed from Michel Foucault, as a particular modality of tackling questions of morality in society. According to her analysis, complex algorithms, such as self-learning neural networks, decenter traditional notions of agency away from human activity, and instead invite posthumanist approaches to agency and morality, as algorithms increase their autopoietic capacity and thus increasingly co-define how human agency is categorized, classified and indeed enabled and restricted. To address this situation, Amoore refers to Foucault's analyses of how individual behavior has been "problematized" (Foucault, 1990, pp. 14–24, 1989 [1984], pp. 295–296) in European antiquity, in the Christian Middle Ages, and in modern European societies—that is, how it has been made the concern of ethical self-conduct in the forefront of systems of normative regulations and moral "code" (Foucault, 1990, *passim*):

> Given a code of actions, and with regard to a specific type of actions (which can be defined by their degree of conformity with or divergence from the code), there are different ways to "conduct oneself" morally, different ways for the acting individual to operate, not just as an agent, but as an ethical subject of this action.
>
> (Foucault, 1990, p. 26)

Accordingly, Amoore uses Foucault's notion of ethics to develop a conception of "cloud ethics" that does not refer to moral systems or individual compliance with these systems but rather to the ways in which human and non-human entities develop a relationship to themselves as actants of self-conduct as they maneuver within their relationships with each other (Foucault, 1989 [1984], p. 296). Her proposal of "cloud ethics" thus aims at rescuing such

DOI: 10.4324/9781003299882-3

potential moments of an ethical "self" from interactions and interdependencies between algorithms and humans, which are usually analyzed in ways that critique the colonization of moral systems through artificial intelligence and interrogate the ways that this colonization pressures individuals into compliant behavior (see, for instance, Rouvroy, 2013; Zuboff, 2015):

> My argument is that there is a need for a certain kind of ethical practice in relation to algorithms, one that does not merely locate the permissions and prohibitions of their use. This different kind of ethical practice begins from the algorithm as always already an ethicopolitical entity by virtue of being immanently formed through the relational attributes of selves and others.
>
> (Amoore, 2020, p. 7)

The algorithms with which this chapter concerns itself are way less complex than those of self-learning neural networks. They make up software that enables what has come to be called Decentralized Finance (DeFi), that is, digital networks of communication, mostly blockchain based, that are designed to circumvent the traditional institutions of finance such as banks, central banks and exchanges, through enabling direct "peer-to-peer" transactions. These algorithms, usually covered by the term "code," are often open source software applications not intended to develop a life of their own and to "learn," but instead to be modified, adapted to new tasks and improved by humans. Still, Amoore's suggestion to use a Foucaultian notion of ethics, as referring to a subjectification through reflective self-conduct as opposed to a mere execution of a system of moral norms, is useful within this chapter's framework. The question is whether and how this kind of "ethics" is possible within contemporary DeFi and the "general purpose technology" of blockchains more generally.

In a nutshell, the chapter approaches this question from the perspective of the unresolvedness of issues of morality and normativity in the field of DeFi. On the one hand, blockchain based DeFi shares with blockchain technologies more generally the refutation of any assumption of preexisting normativity that would govern social coordination as a starting point for suggesting technical solutions to problems of financial coordination. In the proclaimed absence of trust among participants, the technology is meant to provide a technical substitute for that absence. On the other hand, precisely through this DeFi equips the technology with the capacity to induce norm-obedient behavior in participants. Thus, DeFi starts out with the classical sociological *topos* of anomie, laid out by Émile Durkheim (1893), for which then technical solutions are sought, notably through game theoretical designs of code. Given this framework that reifies social norms into technical standards, the question is how something like "cloud ethics," which is based on the Foucaultian understanding that ethics refers to the irreducible individual entity that shapes itself through its relations to others in the forefront of any (moral or technical) "code," is possible at all.

The chapter addresses this question through the following steps, thereby relying both on secondary literature on DeFi and blockchain technologies and on primary sources, such as "whitepapers," through which blockchain and DeFi proponents create their universe of discourse (DuPont & Maurer, 2015). First, DeFi will be characterized as a project of financial micro-coordination. While a micrological view on financial processes is not per se new, given the engagement of the social studies of finance with socio-technical operations on the situational level of financial trading and other financial processes, DeFi differs from traditional finance by explicitly advocating such a micrological view of social coordination. This view makes financial social coordination sociologically visible as imbued with normativity and morality. Second and third, the chapter will reconstruct "anomie" as the basis for the problematization of ethical behavior to be found in DeFi discourses and practices, and the notion of "code" as relating to a modality of morality from which ethics, following Foucault, needs to be distinguished. Fourth, this directs attention to DeFi ethics as crystalizing in the forefront of code. It is a mode of problematizing ethical behavior that concerns itself with the subjective qualities that must be cultivated in order to participate in DeFi in the first place, to stake one's resources in that participation, and to accept its rules and regulations, which are mostly articulated along the lines of game theoretical considerations. In the final analysis, DeFi presents itself as a set of projects that articulate ethical problematizations together with financial rationalities, such as theories of money, the mechanism of the competitive market and the financial transaction as the generic element of social coordination.

Decentralized Finance: Microstructures of Social Coordination

DeFi is a bracket term used to designate financial processes that are not run through the traditional institutions of the financial economy, like stock exchanges, investment banks or central banks, but through blockchain-based transactions of electronic value items directly between participants ('peer-to-peer' transactions). The blockchain technology enables such peer-to-peer transactions through a decentralized modality of accounting, which earmarks each transaction with a singular identification (which in turn allows for the transactors to remain anonymous) that is then recorded on globally distributed electronic "ledgers." At the same time, the term "finance" makes reference to the capacity of contemporary blockchain technology to project financial events, processes and valuations taking place in the institutionalized financial economy into the blockchain universe. This happens through "smart contracts," that is, "on-chain" transaction orders that are affected under the condition that a certain "off-chain" event can be documented to have happened (Caliskan, 2020a). DeFi thus refers not only to a decentralized alternative to traditional financial markets but also to the capacity to process information in those financial markets within the blockchain universe. The point about DeFi is thus to translate off-chain events into on-chain peer-to-peer transactional processes. Thereby, "off" and "on" refer to concrete blockchains, so that an event in one blockchain might constitute an off-chain event for another blockchain.

The peer-to-peer setup of DeFi, replacing centralized financial institutions with direct social coordination among participants, is usually seen as the true revolution of cryptocurrencies, DeFi and blockchain technologies more broadly (Nakamoto, 2008; Buterin, 2014). Yet, traditional financial markets have been described as processes of direct interaction among market participants too, already 20 years ago. Famously, Karin Knorr Cetina and Urs Bruegger (2000, 2002) argued that financial markets are "global microstructures." By this, they mean that those markets, and in particular electronic trading, are based on a social substrate of direct interactions and transactions among market participants. According to their—as has to be admitted, meanwhile dated—empirical characterization of global foreign exchange trading, FX traders in various banks and investment firms directly relate to one another through electronic messenger systems and over the phone in order to orient their actions, to acquire knowledge about market tendencies and to engage in formal and informal reciprocal practices, like such of market making and information exchange. Knorr Cetina and Bruegger argue that financial markets are an important example of a more general tendency in electronically enhanced communication systems, namely, an increase in the importance of situational dynamics, extending from the realm of local face-to-face interactions to financial processes on trans-local scales that do not presuppose a physical co-presence of the interactants. Crucially, this entails the entry of normative considerations and expectations, typical of face-to-face interactions, into financial trading.

The infrastructures of financial markets have thus been described in their micrological quality years before the advent and rise of Bitcoin and DeFi. The difference is, of course, that unlike traditional financial markets, DeFi is openly and devotedly based on the imperative of avoiding centralized institutions (although this claim has been met with doubt, see for a discussion Golumbia, 2016; Parkin, 2019; Caliskan, 2020b) and of dissolving their regulative functions into peer-to-peer transactions. Thus, unlike in traditional financial markets, DeFi's infrastructures are *meant to be* "global microstructures." According to DeFi's ambitions and those of blockchain technologies more generally, they ought to be based on peer-to-peer interactions, taking the form of transactions.

To be sure, these observations cannot ignore critiques that have been put forth against the understanding of (decentralized) finance as a sequence of micrological interactions and transactions. For instance, it has been argued that the thesis of "global microstructures" tends to efface the significance of financial institutions and infrastructures, which have been highlighted by the work of Saskia Sassen (1991, 2005) and others. In this respect, they also tend to miss out on the economic significance of financial markets, taking financial interactions as just another case for the general evolutionary argument of the rise of situational dynamics, including their normative aspects, to global scales (Knorr Cetina, 2009; cf. Langenohl, 2018). With respect to DeFi, and against the background of profound doubt in the realism of claims of complete decentralization of blockchain technologies (Golumbia, 2016; Parkin, 2019), Caliskan (2020b) has argued that the promise of decentralization is challenged through recent tendencies in the reinstitutionalization of blockchain-based financial transactions, in particular, through the rise of quasi-organizations that pool crucial financial functions beyond the enabling of exchange transactions (credit, accounting, exchange between different crypto currencies and between them and fiat currencies, etc.).

Yet in spite of these critiques of viewing finance and DeFi solely through the lens of direct interactions and transactions, it seems important to take the *ambitions* of Defi seriously inasmuch these ambitions become manifested as socio-technical reifications that directly circumscribe the activities of participants, namely, "code." The point is thus not to deny that DeFi does not always, or perhaps at no point, meet the normative expectations it addresses itself with, but to investigate how, and to what extent, these expectations are constitutive of the socio-technical structures that DeFi relies on. Most foundationally, and in contrast to regular financial markets to which the theorem of "global microstructures" has been applied as if it were from the outside, namely from a microsociological and phenomenological perspective, DeFi itself heralds, and is foundationally based on, a *normative* micrological view on financial processes. In other words, notwithstanding criticisms regarding failed decentralization efforts, the micrological quality of DeFi is itself a socio-technically institutionalized result of a certain normative view on finance.

Thus, the question ought to be posed as to how this normative view is founded. As will be argued, that question entails the presence of ethical problematizations among DeFi participants that play a crucial role in the constitution of contemporary DeFi. Thereby, the argumentation unfolds in the following steps. First, DeFi projects will be made visible as confronting themselves with the problem of normlessness in digital financial transactions—a problem that is translated into one of untrustworthy "peers" in peer-to-peer relationships. Second, DeFi projects propose to solve this problem of normlessness and peer untrustworthiness through "code," that is, through software applications whose aim is to ensure that abuse is impossible. Third, however, despite the towering significance of an understanding of morality as (literally) code (to return to Foucault's categories), DeFi also has a place for an ethical modality of morality, that is, for a "problematization" of individuals and their moral self-conduct in decentralized financial settings.

Anomie

The original Bitcoin whitepaper (Nakamoto, 2008) suggested a decentralized ledger for transactions as a solution to the problem of how fraud can be avoided in the settings of online trading, purchasing and digital payments. In particular, the whitepaper argued that an online seller will run the risk of not having the finalization and non-reversibility of the transaction guaranteed, safe through "trusted third parties" (id., p. 1), which will however increase the transaction costs. In other words, the problem to which Bitcoin was suggested as a fix consisted in a so far imperfect solution to the problem of "double spending": namely, that transactors, who in their quality as self-interested individuals could generically not be trusted, could be made to comply only through a centralized institution that did not offer its services for free.

For a sociologist, it is eminent how closely Nakamoto's problem definition resembles that of anomie as in Emile Durkheim (1893), according to whom the main problem of modern, institutionally differentiated societies is the weakening of strong, overarching norms (or "moral" norms, in Durkheim's parlance) guaranteed by normative institutions like law, religion, or state. From the perspective of this analogy, digital decentralization resembles another push of differentiation—namely, the differentiation of "peer to peer" agency from *any* authoritative institution. In the realm of digital payments, anomie takes the form of individual autonomy from normative institutions, resulting in mutual individual untrustworthiness. And in contrast to traditional financial markets, "peer to peer" agency is not normatively stabilized through direct communication among traders who often know each other, as argued by Knorr Cetina and Bruegger (2002), as digital payments among "peers" who may remain anonymous cannot be stabilized through communicative action.

Unlike Durkheim, who had some confidence in the capacity of professional associations to hedge anomie through the reestablishment of collective norms as it was them who were also considered the drivers of institutional differentiation (Durkheim, 1957), Nakamoto sought a technical solution to fix anomie. That technical solution was seen in a peer-to-peer transaction algorithm that would confirm transactions, first, through their individual identifiability, and second, through a process of public accounting in which the majority of users confirmed the transaction through decentrally recording it. The necessity of trust, which could not be guaranteed in the absence of authoritative normative institutions, was to be abolished through enshrining compliance in code. The obvious hope was that normativity, and thus anomie, was an obsolete consideration: If trust was unnecessary because compliance was technically guaranteed, any notion of rule was reduced to that of the architecture of code—that is, of technical standards, not social norms.

From a Foucaultian perspective, software code would thus not only equal moral code but also encompass individual norm-obedient behavior (to which code did not leave any technical alternative) while making redundant any considerations of ethics in the sense of a morally ambiguous relationship of the self to itself. This is at least how it seems at first glance. However, the understandings of "code" in DeFi projects are more complex and ambiguous, leaving room for an ethics of DeFi to emerge.

Code

Ever since the launch of Bitcoin, cryptocurrencies have undergone an evolution that has opened up the possibility to link on-chain transactions with off-chain events, by making on-chain transactions conditional on things going on outside of the respective blockchain. According to Caliskan (2020b), this had the effect of reintroducing centralization processes into DeFi: While on the one hand, on-chain transactions can be connected to numerous events and processes off the respective chain, on the other hand, this requires socio-technical structures that ensure that connectivity. Here, I want to highlight a further consequence of the increasing complexity of on-chain and off-chain processes: namely, the reentry of questions of normativity precisely through the notion of "code."

When Lawrence Lessig published his influential works on "Code is Law" (Lessig, 1999, 2000), blockchain technologies were not yet on the horizon of researchers interested in the effects of algorithmically enabled social orientation. Rather, his interventions, which have been later much quoted by blockchain protagonists (see, for example, DuPont, 2018), referred to the algorithmic governance of the internet technology more broadly. In Lessig, the statement that "code is law" refers to the normative or jurisdictional quality of the programming of internet software. Code enables certain actions while disabling others. It presents users with certain options while withholding others from them. Thus, code has itself a regulatory quality, and that quality must be accounted for. Regulation embodied in code ultimately introduces a normative dimension into the programming of code, which is thus much more than a merely technical affair. At the same time, code itself is unable to account for its normative dimension inasmuch as it presents itself to its users as just a technology. Thus, while code is normative and jurisdictional, by itself it creates no space for negotiating its normative dimensions: "[U]nless we understand how cyberspace can embed, or displace, values from our constitutional tradition, we will lose control over those values. The law in cyberspace—code—will displace them." (Lessig, 2000, n.p.)

This message has not gone amiss in current DeFi projects, which outspokenly take up the normative dimension of jurisdiction through code by enabling collaboration in its development. Blockchain technologies and projects often articulate the ambition that the source code is open and hence can be developed further by all participants (although there are gatekeepers, see Parkin, 2019). Platforms like Ethereum, which perform the connecting between on-chain and off-chain processes, enable users to set up their own code in the construction of smart contracts, so that so-called decentralized autonomous organizations (DAOs) become possible (DuPont, 2018). Moreover, Ethereum stresses the normative dimension inherent in smart contracts by explicitly accounting for the possibility of predatory behavior on the side of users, for instance, by encouraging users to engage with potential loopholes for such behavior in the setup of smart contracts through a training tool called "Capture the Ether."[1]

Smart contracts have also made possible an industry of online ventures developing solutions to what are perceived to be problems or potential problems in smart contracts (like Kleros or Truthcoin). Such problems are seen, for instance, in establishing the status of an off-chain event (e.g., present or absent) so that it can then be transformed into an on-chain transaction. Relatedly, the question is posed of how participants, who are supposed to form the constituency that decides over conflictual matters, can be motivated to "vote" in the case of conflicts over smart contracts (Sztorc, 2015; Lesaege et al., 2018, 2021). Moreover, connections between off-chain events and on-chain transactions are modeled as "prediction markets," which combine Bitcoin's decentralized ledger documentation process with incentives for participants to make trustworthy bets on future events. In the case of the Augur platform, safeguarding the reliability of the betters entails a special sort of "reputation token": "Reputation tokens are gained and lost depending on how reliably their owner votes with the consensus. Reputation holders are obligated to cast a vote every time the network 'checks in' with reality (by default, this is every 8 weeks)." (Peterson & Krug, n.d., p. 2). While these ventures do not necessarily form the core of DeFi, as their ambition is not necessarily to create links between DeFi and traditional finance, they occupy a common discursive space of online interaction and exchange, for instance, through the mutual discussion projects via whitepapers, blogs and specialized periodicals such as *Medium* (DuPont & Maurer, 2015).

We see here that the notion of "code" in DeFi is more complex than it seems at first sight. DeFi promoters react to Lessig's caution against the reification of social norms in software code through an ethos of voluntary participation and collaboration. Code can be modified, and new projects can be begun at any time and, at least in principle, by anybody. In fact, it is through such new projects, forking off from established code, that the number of cryptocurrencies increased so dramatically (see Caliskan, 2020a, p. 541, for recent figures). "Code" thus has a highly complex normative status in DeFi. It is meant to solve the Durkheimian problem of anomie in decentralized social coordination through converting social norms into technical standards and thus to collapse both moral code and moral behavior (*sensu* Foucault) into technical code. But according to the libertarian ethos characterizing DeFi (see Golumbia, 2015), code comes into life only through voluntary participation, be it the participation of software engineers improving code and starting new projects or the participation of DeFi users, who, with the multiplication of cryptocurrencies and related financial services (see Caliskan, 2020b), have to find motivation to engage in particular DeFi projects. It is here, I argue, that ethics, understood with Foucault as the conduct of self, comes into play.

Ethics

Foucault argues, on the example of the Greek and Roman ethics of the conduct of the self regarding the "use of pleasures," that ethics was "was a means of developing—for the smallest minority of the population, made up of free, adult males—an aesthetics of existence, the purposeful art of a freedom perceived as a power game" (Foucault, 1990, p. 253). Ethics is a mode of morality that forms as the consequence of problematizations of moral subjecthood, whose condition of possibility is the absence of a moral code that would authoritatively prescribe moral agency (Foucault, 1989 [1984], pp. 298–299, 1990, pp. 25–32). Hence, the principal freedom of the individual—notably including the freedom of the other (Foucault, 1990, p. 252)—is the precondition for ethics. The ethical reflection "spoke to them [free Greek men] concerning precisely those conducts in which they were called upon to exercise their rights, their power, their authority, and their liberty" (Foucault, 1990, p. 23)." I argue that the possibility for such an ethical problematization under conditions of decentralized social coordination, as in DeFi, manifests itself as a consequence of a libertarian understanding of agency and social coordination, whose notion of the individual freedom of self and other establishes a tension and a counterweight to the techno-moral notion of "code" characterizing blockchain ventures. The rest of this section will dissect how DeFi ethics emerges in the forefront of "code" and in non-overlap with it—at least transitorily, that is, as long as DeFi is still in an emergent state and has not yet attained the quality of a system conditioning any financial agency.

The first ethical forefront of code concerns the question of why individuals should actually find it useful or desirable to engage in practices of decentralized social (here: financial) coordination whose risks have been so elaborately articulated by the critics of cryptocurrencies and DeFi (Golumbia, 2015, 2016; Eich, 2019; Parkin, 2019, 2020). Opting for DeFi is a decision that code itself cannot guarantee. A certain conduct of the self is required to engage in these practices. A first dimension of this conduct of self is the *cultivation of distrust*, both in centralized institutions and in the "peers" that DeFi brings together. While the Bitcoin whitepaper addresses distrust in decentralized digital payment systems as a self-evident matter, distrust, sociologically speaking, is not a matter of course at all. To some degree, "trust" can be regarded as a functional substitute for complete knowledge, enabling actors to engage in agency without fully knowing its preconditions and consequences (Lewis & Weigert, 1985). In this sense, trust is also economically superior to knowledge because it requires fewer resources to enable agency. Thus, to embrace distrust requires an additional framing that problematizes trust as a generic attitude and renders its cost visible. In the Bitcoin whitepaper (Nakamoto, 2008), this is done through the instilment of uncertainty regarding the finality of a financial transaction (a digital payment), which works along the lines of two invocations of utilitarian rationality. The subjects *ought not* to trust in centralized institutions because these don't offer their services for free and are beyond the individual's control; and the subjects *must not* trust their peers because they will use any opportunity to spend their coins more than once. Thus, the technical solution that Bitcoin proposes to the "double-spending problem" (id., p. 1), which arises only as a combination of that double invocation or utilitarian rationality, articulates a problematization of ethical conduct, that is, of a relationship of the subject to itself in the midst of relationships it entertains to others. It is necessary for the subjects to simultaneously cultivate a distrust both in central institutions and in their transactional peers in order to generate a motivation for engaging in DeFi in the first place.

With the advent of smart contracts that allow for the integration of on-chain and off-chain processes, epitomized by Ethereum, the problematization of ethical conduct in the forefront of code has multiplied. This is because smart contracts enable much more than the establishment of new cryptocurrencies, namely, so-called decentralized autonomous organizations (DAOs) that can be attuned to virtually any aim technically commensurable with decentralized ledger documentation. A precondition for this is a membership in the platform, consisting basically of holding a digital "wallet" containing value tokens of the platform's currency (in the case of Ethereum, "ethers"). Hence, DAOs can be regarded as conditional on some engagement of their participants in DeFi—they are contingent upon financial *investment*. I argue that this creates another ethical forefront of code in DeFi. Motivation to engage in smart contract design and DAOs is not only (as has been remarked upon in the literature, DuPont, 2018; Parkin, 2019) an affair of social stratification as voting power ultimately depends on stock in crypto assets. More foundationally, motivation rests on a decision to dedicate one's financial resources to a particular venture, and hence to cultivate a utilitarian interest in that venture. The ethics thus circumscribed might be termed *entrepreneurial*: The relationship of self to itself and to others and the attitude to be cultivated in these relationships link expenditure to the formation of interest in a particular venture. According to the research literature, this entrepreneurial ethics often assumes a game-changing ambition, promising no less than horizontal solutions for protracted and wicked problems such as environmental damages (DuPont, 2018).

The two ethical forefronts of code discussed so far emerge from the freedom of the individual to (not) engage in DeFi, and consequently form around problematizations of motivation for such engagement. Thereby, two things must be noted. First, read through a sociologist's glasses, DeFi ethics responds to the Durkheimian problem of anomie with a Parsonsian conception of socialization into norms through the generation of motivation. Adding an agency-theoretic dimension borrowed from Max Weber to Durkheim' diagnosis of anomie, Talcott Parsons argued that individuals are enabled through socialization not only to execute norms but to embrace them (Parsons & Shils, 1959). In other words, he enriched Durkheim's notion of norm as urge and pressure with an element of motivation and identification. This is also the conceptual architecture of DeFi ethics. In the postulated absence of trust and normativity, DeFi holds individuals capable of generating motivation for engaging in decentralized financial processes all the same, provided that they engage in a certain cultivation of relations to self and others as described above. Second, the problematization of ethical conduct is constitutively based on financial processes and rationalities. This pertains in particular to the acceptance of a certain theory of digital money (namely, as the circulation of identifiable "coins" that bears some resemblance to commodity theories of money, Bjerg, 2015) and to an entrepreneurial attitude that couples motivation with initiative investment, usually referred to as venture capital.

The third problematization of ethical conduct in DeFi addresses the potential agency of DeFi participants once they have chosen to commit themselves to DeFi. This is where code in the narrower sense enters the scene of problematization, because code is meant to solve a problem that emanates from DeFi's libertarian ideology. This problem consists of an outspokenly morally ambivalent notion of individual and individual interest. On the one hand, DeFi accepts, actually embraces, the capacity of people to pursue their own interests without the interference of authoritative institutions; their self-interest is not to be circumscribed by any such institution. On the other hand, this means that digital decentralized action coordination also has to accept the potentially problematic aspects of such unrestrained utilitarian individualism—which, in the parlance of many whitepapers, is "greed" (cf. Nakamoto, 2008, p. 4; Sztorc, 2015, p. 1). The same utilitarian individual that is celebrated as the moral anchor of DeFi becomes the major problem for decentralized social coordination—hence the insistence on the necessity of a "trustless" system of social coordination, to be enabled through code as that which reifies norms into technical standards.

I argue that this problematization of the autonomous yet potentially greedy individual carries with it an ethical *urgence*. That is to say, an individual needs to develop and cultivate a certain attitude toward herself before being able to accept the subjugation to code (which is itself a highly contested field in DeFi, see DuPont, 2018). To begin with, she needs to accept, and embrace, the negative anthropology of decentralized libertarianism in order to receive a justification for subjecting herself to code. This is exemplified through a conflict, described by DuPont (2018), among an Ethereum-based DAO's constituency over an abuse of their crowd fund through a participant that was inadvertently enabled by code. While some participants argued for a reversal of the process through retroactively forking the chain, others accepted, even embraced, the abuse as something that could not be messed with as it was made possible by code ('code is law' being their motto). Accepting greed and abuse as normalcy correlates with accepting code as an indisputable, quasi-natural law.

However, the implications of the acceptance of this negative anthropology go further. They find expression in the definite propensity of DeFi projects to use game theory in order to devise their code. A typical and often cited reference is Thomas Schelling's (1960) notion of "cooperative games." These are games in which actors have a positive incentive to align their expectations with those of other actors, as failing to meet those others' expectations will result in the withholding of gratification. The classical example in Schelling is the task to meet with another person in a city while knowing only the time of the meeting, not the location. Schelling argues that under such conditions, and without the possibility to directly communicate with each other, participants will have an incentive to take the perspective of the other person and to consider what that other person might consider as an appropriate meeting place, or what they might consider to be their own considerations regarding such a place. For Schelling, this constitutes an incentive to "agree" on a meeting place, or on any other matter, with the other person (id., pp. 54–57, 89–99).

DeFi projects refer to this type of game in order to provide solutions for the problem of how compliant behavior can be guaranteed at the interface between on-chain and off-chain processes, be it through smart contracts (as in Kleros, cf. Lesaege et al., 2021) or through prediction markets (as in Augur, Peterson & Krug, n.d.) or a combination of both (as in Truthcoin, Sztorc, 2015). For exemplification, I will elaborate on Lithium Finance (2021), a DeFi venture whose business model is to provide pricing information about illiquid assets. These are assets that are not traded on exchanges and for which no market price information is thus available (e.g., companies in private proprietorship; Lithium Finance, 2021). Like the Augur platform (Peterson & Krug, n.d.), Lithium sets up a prediction market for this kind of information. "Price seekers" will announce a premium on correct and reliable information regarding the pricing of a certain illiquid asset, and "price experts" (also termed "wisdom nodes") will share their opinion regarding the virtual market price of that asset and receive (parts of) the premium if their information is considered accurate.[2]

Thereby, the price experts operate under the following conditions. First, the accuracy of the information is not primarily confirmed through external information (for instance, accounting data) or through a later actual market price (say, after an IPO), but through establishing the relation between the individual piece of information and (broadly speaking) the market opinion. This is owed to a prediction market rationality, which presupposes, following Hayek (1978), that competitive markets optimally pool all available information and transform it into a single figure of maximum commensurability (the price) that is then considered the most accurate information possible (Abramowicz, 2008). Second, price experts can increase the impact of their price guesses through staking value tokens (called $Lith), which likewise follows a prediction market logic that high-stake bets are more reliable than low-stake ones (Abramowicz, 2008). Third, price experts may gain or lose reputation tokens, depending on how accurate (in the above sense) their guesses are, which will be recorded on Lithium's blockchain ledger.

Thus, the incentive structure that Lithium proposes is designed to solve the problem of the reliability of price informants at the interface between off-chain world (information on the value of illiquid assets) and on-chain transactions (the prediction market and the mechanisms of gratification, punishment and decentralized ledger documentation built around it). However, this architecture of incentives implies a crucially ethical scene: namely, that the individuals *stake* their contributions—in the case of lithium, in order to signal the confidentiality of their pricing guesses. Just as Foucault held regarding the Greek erotic ethics, there is no law or code that authoritatively prescribes a certain behavior. Individuals can decide for themselves if and how much they stake. Yet, the market mechanism that pools their information urges them to look at themselves as if through the market's eye and to cultivate a certain ethics of staking one's claims in the presence of a universalist anthropology that individuals are not trustworthy—including oneself. And again, just as mentioned before, this ethical problematization is bound up with and rests upon financial rationalities—in the case of staking claims, voting and so on, the rationality of a prediction market that operates on transactions as elementary particles of social coordination.

Conclusion: The Future Vanishing of DeFi Ethics

This paper has argued that the ethical dimension of blockchain and algorithm-powered DeFi resides in a complex interplay of different modalities of morality, as distinguished by Michel Foucault. Among these is ethics as the development of a relationship to oneself and others geared at the cultivation of a conduct that counts as moral without being adamantly prescribed by norms or fully inculcated into individuals through discipline. In this sense, ethics in DeFi, while referring to software code as that which enables the new financial technologies, operates in the forefront of code, understood both as a technical and as a normative set of rules and procedures.

Accordingly, DeFi can be understood, and actually understands itself, as a set of projects that proceeds from a Durkheimian problem of anomie: how is social coordination possible in the absence of effective normative rules? The way that DeFi addresses this problem is not only through the development of software code that enshrines normative expectations into technical standards but also through the combination of code as technically reified norms that cannot be breached with the problematization of a libertarian subject that is required to position herself vis-à-vis code.

The problematization of this self-conduct, which is ethics in the Foucaultian sense, plays a functional role in the setup of DeFi. First, it is a prerequisite for imagining and advocating participation in decentralized social coordination, through the necessary cultivation of a distrust in central institutions and the "peer" others. Second, it is a way to smooth over the glaring ideological contradictions between naturalized code and libertarian understandings of freedom. Potentially unethical behavior is problematized in order to justify code (designed according to game theory) as its forced solution while retaining the possibility to opt in and out of the system and to actively embrace its norms.

It is absolutely possible that the ethical moment in Defi vanishes as soon as DeFi becomes a systemic environment for financial agency, in which case motivation for engagement in it will be generated by the system itself, that is, its unavoidability. Such a development would write forth Max Weber's (2001) account of the vanishment of the requirement of a "protestant ethic" as a motivational source for engaging in capitalism as soon as capitalism transforms itself into the condition of possibility for any economic agency.

Thus, ethical problematization, in the sense of Foucault, might turn out to be a transient phenomenon in an emerging digital sociotechnical arrangement of financial coordination, and its current presence might be owed to the still emergent stage of DeFi and digital decentralized social coordination. What, however, is most probably here to stay is the financial underpinnings of DeFi ethics. DeFi ethics is articulated along the lines of financial rationalities, like money theories, the mechanics of competitive markets and the valorization of transactions as elementary particles of any social coordination.

Notes

1 Retrieved July 4, 2022, from https://capturetheether.com/
2 See the current whitepaper. Retrieved July 4, 2022, from https://docs.lith.finance/ and the earlier Litepaper (Lithium Finance, 2021).

References

Abramowicz, M. (2008). *Predictocracy: Market mechanisms for public and private decision making*. Yale University Press.

Amoore, L. (2020). *Cloud ethics: Algorithms and the attributes of ourselves and others*. Duke University Press.

Bjerg, O. (2015). How is bitcoin money? *Theory, Culture & Society*, *33*(1), 53–72.

Buterin, V. (2014). *Ethereum: A next-generation smart contract and decentralized application platform*. www.ethereum.org

Caliskan, K. (2020a). Data money: The socio-technical infrastructure of cryptocurrency blockchains. *Economy and Society*, *49*(4), 540–561.

Caliskan, K. (2020b). Platform works as stack economization: Cryptocurrency markets and exchanges in perspective. *Sociologica*, *14*(3), 115–142.

DuPont, Q. (2018). Experiments in algorithmic governance: A history and ethnography of "the DAO," a failed decentralized autonomous organization. In M. Campbell-Verduyn (Ed.), *Bitcoin and beyond* (pp. 157–177). Routledge.

DuPont, Q., & Maurer, B. (2015). *Ledgers and law in the blockchain*. UC Irvine. Retrieved September 16, 2021, from https://escholarship.org/uc/item/6k65w4h3

Durkheim, É. (1957). *Professional ethics and civic morals*. Routledge & Kegan Paul.

Durkheim, É. (2013 [1893]). *The division of labour in society* (S. Lukes, Ed. and with a new Intro., & W. D. Halls, Trans.). Palgrave Macmillan.

Eich, S. (2019). Old Utopias, new tax havens: The politics of bitcoin in historical perspective. In P. Hacker, I. Lianos, G. Dimitropoulos, & S. Eich (Eds.), *Regulating blockchain: Techno-social and legal challenges* (pp. 85–98). Oxford University Press. https://doi.org/10.1093/oso/9780198842187.003.0005

Foucault, M. (1989 [1984]). The concern for truth. In S. Lotringer (Ed.) & J. Johnston (Trans.), *Foucault live (interviews, 1966–84)* (pp. 293–308). Semiotext(e).

Foucault, M. (1990). *The use of pleasure: The history of sexuality* (Vol. 2, R. Hurley, Trans. from the French). Vintage Books.

Golumbia, D. (2015). Bitcoin as politics: Distributed right-wing extremism. In G. Lovink, N. Tkacz, & P. De Vries (Eds.), *Moneylab reader: An intervention in digital economy*. Institute of Network Cultures.

Golumbia, D. (2016). Computerization always promotes centralization even as it promotes decentralization. In R. Simanowski (Ed.), *Digital humanities and digital media: Conversations on politics, culture aesthetics and literacy* (pp. 123–147). Open Humanities Press.

Hayek, F. A. V. (1984 [1978]): Competition as a discovery procedure. In: C. Nishiyama & K. R. Leube (Eds.), *The essence of Hayek* (pp. 254–265). Hoover Institution Press.

Knorr Cetina, K. (2009). The synthetic situation: Interactionism for a global world. *Symbolic Interaction*, *32*(1), 61–87.

Knorr Cetina, K., & Bruegger, U. (2000). The market as an object of attachment: Exploring postsocial relations in financial markets. *Canadian Journal of Sociology*, *25*(2), 141–168.

Knorr Cetina, K., & Bruegger, U. (2002). Traders' engagement with markets: A postsocial relationship. *Theory, Culture & Society*, *19*(5–6), 161–185.

Langenohl, A. (2018). Financial markets as interpretive economies: An overview of the meaning of financialized money. In D. Cuonz, J. Metelmann, & S. Loren (Eds.), *Screening economies: Money matters and the ethics of representation* (pp. 25–140). Transcript.

Lesaege, C., & George, W. (2018). Kleros and Augur—keeping people honest on the blockchain through game theory. *Medium*. Retrieved September 14, 2021, from https://medium.com/kleros/kleros-and-augur-keeping-people-honest-on-ethereum-through-game-theory-56210457649c

Lesaege, C., George, W., & Ast, F. (2021). Kleros: Long paper v2.0.2. *Kleros*. Retrieved September 14, 2021, from https://kleros.io/yellowpaper.pdf

Lessig, L. (1999). *Code and other laws of cyberspace*. Basic Books.

Lessig, L. (2000). Code is law: On liberty in cyberspace. *Harvard Magazine*. Retrieved July 4, 2022, from www.harvardmagazine.com/2000/01/code-is-law-html

Lewis, J. D., & Weigert, A. (1985). Trust as a social reality. *Social Forces*, *63*(4), 967–985.

Lithium Finance (2021). Lithium finance litepaper v1. *Lithium Finance*. Retrieved September 14, 2021, from https://lith.finance/#litepaper

Nakamoto, S. (2008). *Bitcoin: A peer-to-peer electronic cash system*. www.bitcoin.org

Parkin, J. (2019). The senatorial governance of bitcoin: Making (de)centralized money. *Economy and Society*, *48*(4), 463–487. https://doi.org/10.1080/03085147.2019.1678262

Parkin, J. (2020). *Money/code/space: Bitcoin, blockchain, and geographies of algorithmic decentralisation*. Oxford University Press.

Parsons, T., & Shils, E. W. (1959). Some fundamental categories of the theory of action: A general statement. In *Toward a general theory of action* (pp. 3–29). Harvard University Press.

Peterson, J., & Krug, J. (n.d.). *Augur: A decentralized, open-source platform for prediction markets*. Retrieved September 4, 2021, from www.augur.net

Rouvroy, A. (2013). The end(s) of critique: Data behaviourism versus due process. In M. Hildebrandt & K. de Vries (Eds.), *Privacy, due process and the computational turn: The philosophy of law meets the philosophy of technology*. Routledge.

Sassen, S. (1991). *The global city: New York, London, Tokyo*. Princeton University Press.

Sassen, S. (2005). The embeddedness of electronic markets: The case of global capital markets. In K. Knorr Cetina & A. Preda (Eds.), *The sociology of financial markets* (pp. 17–37). Oxford University Press.

Schelling, T. C. (1960). *The strategy of conflict*. Oxford University Press.

Sztorc, P. (2015). Truthcoin: Peer-to-peer oracle system and prediction marketplace. *Truthcoin*. Retrieved September 14, 2021, from www.truthcoin.info/papers/truthcoin-whitepaper.pdf

Weber, M. (2001 [1907]). *The protestant ethic and the spirit of capitalism* (T. Parsons, Trans., & A. Giddens, Intro.). Routledge.

Zuboff, S. (2015). Big other: Surveillance capitalism and the prospects of an information civilization. *Journal of Information Technology*, *30*, 75–89.

4 Audio Beacon Technologies, Surveillance and the Digital Paradox

Julian Iliev

Overview

Audio beacons are hidden inside digital devices. They emit and receive high-frequency audio signals that are inaudible to the human ear, thereby generating and transmitting data without our knowledge. The research takes an interdisciplinary approach involving (1) a survey of audio beacon technology, (2) a contextualization in terms of contemporary theories of surveillance and control and (3) an interpretation in terms of 20th-century dystopian literature. Finally, this research introduces the notion of a *digital paradox* in which the dystopian worlds of George Orwell and Aldous Huxley are brought together in order to characterize surveillance and control in contemporary society.

Audio Beacon Technologies

A few different names are used to represent the same audio beacon framework: ultrasound beacons, data over audio and uBeacons. Audio beacon technologies utilize a range of sounds between 18 kHz and 20 kHz (Arp et al., 2017, p. 35). These high-frequency sounds possess triple benefits—they are inaudible to humans, they are detected by other devices, and they have diminished interference with the human voice. As such, "ultrasound . . . is a perfect match for designing an inaudible yet effective side channel between devices" (Arp et al., 2017, p. 37). Audio beacons require a speaker and a microphone to transmit. All mobile devices contain these two components, and they can transmit sound up to 44 kHz (Vaghasiya et al., 2018, p. 413; Arp et al., 2017, p. 35). Audio beacons do not require additional hardware, nor do they depend on Wi-Fi, Bluetooth or network connectivity (Vaghasiya et al., 2018, p. 416; Arp et al., 2017, p. 37). The frequencies between 18 kHz and 20 kHz are divided into smaller units, and a character or a symbol is assigned to each one of those units (Mavroudis et al., 2017, p. 100). Thus, audio beacons are able to transmit characters or symbols.

This framework can be installed into any mobile app, which can play the inaudible sound unbeknownst to the user and simultaneously be detectable by

DOI: 10.4324/9781003299882-4

other microphones. A business owner can embed audio beacon technologies into their app without explicit disclosure. After the uBeacon is embedded, the app is made available for customer downloads. The first time the app is activated, a request asking for microphone permission is displayed. Granting the app permission to use the microphone in turn activates the audio beacon technology. The users are not aware when the microphone is being used or the type of data transmitted to a server (Arp et al., 2017, p. 35), nor are they notified that the app will listen in the background (Mavroudis et al., 2017, p. 100). The information transmitted includes device identity, phone model, IMEI, OS version, location, behavior of the user and other devices present (Arp et al., 2017, pp. 36, 38, 40). Moreover, audio beacon technologies have access to all audible frequencies and are listening "even when the application has not been 'manually' started by the user" (Mavroudis et al., 2017, p. 100). There are only two ways of stopping the invasive framework: delete the app or decline microphone permission.

Audio Beacon Capabilities

Audio beacons have multiple capabilities: location tracking, cross-device identification, de-anonymization and media tracking. They can trigger actions on a mobile device without user consent.

Location Tracking

Arp et al. (2017) examine three companies: Lisnr, Shopkick and Silverpush. The first two companies use audio beacons in mobile apps for location tracking, while Silverpush uses inaudible sound for media monitoring and cross-device tracking. Mavroudis et al. (2017) add a few more businesses to the list of audio beacon companies: Google Cast, CopSonic, Signal360, Audible Magic (pp. 95–96). These apps are listening for ultrasonic beacons in the background without user awareness, and they transmit location data without the use of GPS (Arp et al., 2017, p. 36). When we work with precise location accuracy (less than 10 cm), other dimensions can be established. By implementing algorithms in combination with educated guesses, one can deduce users' actions and activities.

Ashbrook and Starner (2003) have developed an algorithm that successfully predicts the future movement of users based on location tracking. The researchers were able to deduce significant locations for each user based on the previous two locations visited. They were also able to predict the behavior of the users, their next destination and if certain individuals were going to meet. The results of the research show that the algorithm worked with both single and multi-user prediction and "showed relative frequencies significantly greater than chance" (Ashbrook & Starner, 2003, p. 285). Facebook had identical research in their patent called "Offline Trajectories" (Heerden et al., 2019, p. 2). Based on user location and Facebook data, the company was able to predict the future movement of individuals. Thus, location data (regardless of how it is generated) largely predicts human behavior and the collection of location data allows companies to predict what a user is going to do next, before the users themselves may know.

Cross-device Identification

Devices emitting audio beacons continuously detect other devices in the vicinity. It's simple to deduce that those devices belong to the same individual. Thus, the behavior of users can be monitored across multiple devices. Further, the information establishes a connection between work and personal devices, which has privacy and security implications as well. The Chief Marketing Officer and co-founder of Silverpush, Mudit Seth, confirms this by saying, "We are able to match 70 to 80 percent of desktop users to their mobile phones" (Taslima, 2014, p. 108).

De-anonymization

The implementation of audio beacons allows de-anonymization for Bitcoin and Tor users. The ultrasonic signal can establish a connection between the real location of the device, the actual user and the Bitcoin address. This reveals the individual's identity (Arp et al., 2017, p. 37). The same is true for Tor and VPN users (Mavroudis et al., 2017, p. 96). De-anonymization is made possible by the beacon's continuous listening mode, which captures human voices. Mavroudis et al. (2017) uncover the vulnerability of ultrasonic technologies to de-anonymization attacks, not only by the companies that manufacture them but by third parties as well (p. 102).

Media Tracking

Silverpush is aiming to track users' TV viewing habits. The ultrasound beacon can transmit watched content data, including time, location, broadcast channel and the duration of the viewing. Thus, the viewing behavior of the individual is connected to their mobile devices. Highly sensitive viewing habits of individuals (religious, political, medical and sexual) can be revealed across multiple devices and locations (Arp et al., 2017, p. 36).

Trigger Actions

Vaghasiya et al. (2018) propose an inaudible beacon triggering system (pp. 414, 418). Sounds emitted by any speaker lasting only 0.0005 to 0.002 seconds can trigger predetermined actions on a smartphone without any interaction with the user. The sound can be played on a loop continuously, or when the desired action is required. One transmission can activate multiple devices. The actions can display an advertisement, push notifications or load a predetermined web page. More invasive actions include changing sound profiles, enabling location tracking and Wi-Fi and Bluetooth toggling. The researchers claim that their system can be employed in speakers, shopping malls, TV and radio commercials, children's toys, classrooms, concerts and public spaces (Vaghasiya et al., 2018, pp. 414–416). It can also be embedded into any mobile phone application and even function in airplane mode. The proposed system also keeps a history log of all the triggering activities and transmits it to the local server (Vaghasiya et al., 2018, p. 415). As the researchers state, "This kind of implementation by marketers can not only provide rich and immersive experience but also help them with user tracking and analytics" (Vaghasiya et al., 2018, p. 417).

The ethical implications of the above stated capabilities will be explored in the following sections. John Sullins (2010) even highlights computer ethics as the "primary concern of our time" (p. 130). Cross-device identification and de-anonymization have dire consequences for an individual's privacy and for freedom of speech activists as is evident in the case of Chinese whistleblower Shi Tao (Sullins, 2010, p. 116). An app that changes the preferred settings on our mobile device without user permission is unquestionably invasive. But it also changes the meaning of *personal device*.

Lonneke van der Velden (2015) distinguishes two ways that digital devices transmit information: insertion and leakage (p. 183). Insertion is when the NSA implants malware in the digital devices of users they want to monitor. Leakage is the assembly of prodigious personal data from phone calls, text messages, social media, search queries, website traffic and third-party aggregated data (Van der Velden, 2015, p. 186). It is not random that the terms are sexually suggestive. All data is intimate and unique to the user. Leaking data is not a secondary feature of audio beacon technologies, but rather their intended purpose. The data can be used against the data generator, so audio beacons are self-implicating technologies. They leak information by design, which reverses the definition of "personal device."

Van der Velden (2015) states that digital devices "lead their own life" (p. 189), and they do not belong to the user entirely. I would expand by saying that technologies implementing audio beacons are personal, but not because we own them, rather because they transmit personal data. The capabilities of audio beacon technologies not only result in loss of privacy, but they also nourish surveillance and expand power imbalance.

Introduction to Surveillance

Surveillance involves the act of looking at or listening to a specific person, event or situation. This act of observation is not innocuous. Instead, the observer strives to collect detailed data, identify correlations and assemble the data into meaningful units. For example, parents monitor their children in their cribs with audio devices. These audio-video tools are the norm. As the child grows, this mode of observation will incorporate continual behavior corrections by the parents. The child is molded to learn and perform the proper behaviors that society expects, as well as obeying cultural norms. This mode of observation analysis and parental critique intensifies with age. Teenagers can be subjected to parental controls on their digital devices, and parents may choose a more severe form of surveillance by installing tracking apps on their children's phones. Paradoxically, this stage of quiet surveillance also winds its tentacles around the parents at their workplace. The rabbit hole continues endlessly as the people who monitor the workers are monitored themselves by someone else. Thus, surveillance asserts a power structure charged with hierarchy and control.

The Importance of Audio Surveillance

The question arises—Is audio spying necessary when video cameras are present?

The research on audio histograms by Reddy et al. (2014) states—"Human beings express their emotions like happiness, sadness, anger, panic, shock, and surprising events in terms of different forms of speech . . . Hence, most of the acoustic events in human presence can be detected from the speech signals" (p. 1978). Further, the research by Crocco et al. (2016) finds real world video surveillance not to be sufficient and reliable enough if it's used alone without the support of additional sensory trackers. Video surveillance has been strongly enhanced with audio, while audio-only devices continue to be implemented as a separate surveillance strategy.

While video tends to record our external state, audio discloses the intimacy of our internal state. Health conditions may be revealed as well as mental state and live dreams. Consequently, audio data becomes more valuable than ocular data. There are five other practical reasons: (1) audio requires less bandwidth and storage, (2) omni-directional microphones capture audio 360 degrees, (3) audio bounces off of surfaces allowing capture despite obstacles, (4) strong light and temperature are not concerns and (5) incidents involving screams are undetectable when out of view (Crocco et al., 2016, p. 2). Gary Marx (1998) calls this contemporary all-encompassing mode of surveillance a "new surveillance" (p. 172). He argues that the governmental data protection model as stated by the fair information practice of 1973 is inadequate because it does not take into consideration the ethical aspect of data collection. This inadequacy is enhanced by the robust capabilities of the new technologies (Marx, 1998, p. 172).

Web of Surveillance

Although research has shown that big data companies are able to manipulate elections (Tufekci, 2014; Zittrain, 2014), designating them as the sinister Big

Brother requires a giant leap. Ergo, individuals rarely see the value of their own data. Luke Stark (2016) defines this blind spot of perception as "data myopia" (p. 21). Data myopia prevails because individuals do not comprehend how their data grows or witness any negative consequences because companies are not disclosing how they are using the data. Effectively, people fail to form a crucial bond with their own data (Stark, 2016, p. 21), allowing a state of data capitalism to develop (West, 2019, p. 20).

Sarah West (2019) views this data aggregation of gestures and utterances as an imbalanced territory with an "asymmetric redistribution of power" (p. 20). These conditions enable the growth and the advancement of corporations, which expand capital and motivate the development of additional invasive technologies. Consumer data is valued by the existence of data brokers who buy and resell the commodity (West, 2019, p. 31). Companies' methods of attaining personal data are not available for examination, personal consent or legal action because the practice is hidden from public view (Zuboff, 2015, p. 78). Surveillance and tracking technologies create environments where the individual is unfailingly visible, or, as Haggerty and Ericson (2000) coin, the state of "disappearance of disappearance" (p. 619). The commerce of personal data is facilitated by the free market economy, which then enables data aggregation within the same organization (private, public or governmental). This data gives the organization a comprehensive picture of the user. Implementing this knowledge, the business can manipulate individuals to further their own agenda. With this capability, Big Brother has just become a small step within the organization's culture.

Surveillance Societies

Foucault (1995) finds surveillance to be an integral aspect of the disciplinary power structure (p. 175). Surveillance monitors production inside the given environment, but more importantly, it is a hierarchic network (Foucault, 1995, p. 177). In a sovereign society (approximately, 18th century), the ruler is visible and exhibits detailed documentation of his deeds as an "account of his life" (Foucault, 1995, p. 191). Documentation of his look, description of his mannerisms and the written record of his daily activities are a privilege bestowed on the worthy. Disciplinary societies not only reverse this trend but also adjust the meaning of visibility by turning it into "means of control and a method of domination" (Foucault, 1995, p. 191). In a disciplinary society (approximately, 19th century and the beginning of the 20th century), power structures remain unseen, while people have to be constantly visible. In addition, the person's individuality must be uncovered, because that knowledge guarantees their subordination and objectification. Foucault concludes that *discipline* is an intricate system comprised of various techniques and mechanisms that identify *discipline* as power. As such, in the disciplinary society, there is a preoccupation with the organization, classification and normalization of the populace executed with the aid of documentation and "statistical methods" (Cohen, 2008, p. 185). Records were "both a technique of power and a procedure of knowledge" (Foucault, 1995, p. 148) that produced individuals "as objects and as instruments" (Foucault, 1995, p. 170). The production of norms, which necessitate the individual's proper behavior, becomes the main goal (Galic et al., 2017, pp. 16–17).

Gilles Deleuze (1992) observes that the disciplinary societies transitioned to *societies of control* by the mid-20th century (pp. 3–4). If large buildings (schools, hospitals, military barracks, factories and prisons) are characteristic of the disciplinary society, then the corporation is the embodiment of the societies of control (Deleuze, 1992, p. 4). In societies of control, Deleuze (1992) finds the individual has become a *dividual*—a digital representation of a person (p. 5). A dividual is the accumulation of digital traces resembling a person, not an individual of flesh and blood. Thus, the interest shifts from the physical body to the online behavior and resulting digital traces. These are combined later in separate settings to form what Haggerty and Ericson (2000) call *data doubles* (p. 606). The data doubles are examined in different environments (governmental, financial and health institutions) to devise procedures of control, so the data doubles are an "additional self" (Galic et al., 2017, p. 22). In computer-based design fields, a similar concept is called the *digital twin*—"a virtual representation of a physical object or process capable of collecting information from the real environment to represent, validate and simulate the physical twin's present" (Botin-Sanabria et al., 2022, p. 1).

Haggerty and Ericson (2000) see the formation of virtual data doubles yielding two additional features: (1) the combination of digital traces offers increased understanding of the individual and (2) multiplies the strength of the surveillance. They coin the term *surveillance assemblage* to represent the combination of various data streams that work together when assembled (Haggerty & Ericson, 2000, p. 608). The prime motive is to gather large amounts of data to intimately understand the subject. After the information is received, it is reassembled at multiple institutions. The data doubles are investigated, and a plan is implemented for control or intervention. In that sense, Haggerty and Ericson agree that surveillance assemblage is closely connected to Orwell's portrayal in *Nineteen Eighty-Four* and more dissimilar to Foucault's panopticon.

Audio beacons collect personal data by direct and indirect observation. Meaning the information collected and transmitted can directly identify a person, their surroundings and others in the vicinity, while simultaneously collecting data indirectly, because the subject is unaware it's happening. Location tracking and de-anonymization of audio beacon technologies enable a state of full visibility, which contributes to the power imbalance. This environment resembles societies of control where supervision and control are implemented by digital devices. The ability of audio beacon technologies to locate and broadcast the position of any user at any time resembles surveillance akin to an "electronic collar" (Deleuze, 1992, p. 7). This digital collar surpasses previous surveillance technologies through mass transmission of audio data, thus allowing large scale surveillance.

Implementation

To address the socio-economic implications related to the implementation of audio beacon technologies, I will explore their active realization in applications that are widely used in our digital society. The research by Arp et al. (2017) focuses on three companies developing those technologies: Lisnr, Shopkick and Silverpush.

The Cincinnati-based start-up, Lisnr, has been partners with VISA since 2015, and recently the credit card giant has invested more capital in the company (Butler, 2019). In addition to VISA, Lisnr has partnered with Ticketmaster for processing ticket scanning, transacting payments and cell phone authentication. Lisnr has also partnered with the music band Swedish House Mafia, singer J. Cole and Budweiser Made in America tour and are collaborators with Jay-Z's record label (Flynn, 2014). In all these situations, Lisnr is using their algorithm for transactions based on audio, but that function does not replace the capabilities discussed previously: location tracking, de-anonymization and cross-device identification. Case in point, Lisnr has also partnered with Jaguar Land Rover for customization of automobile settings (Rehbock, 2017). Lisnr claims that they can determine and differentiate who the driver of the vehicle is and who the passenger is. Additional partners that Lisnr is working with are listed on the company's website and include Intel, Synchrony, MIO and SAP.

The second audio beacon development company listed, Shopkick, is venturing into the retail market. They are working with retailers such as American Eagle, Sports Authority (Slade, 2014), Macy's, Target (Forbes, 2021) and ExxonMobil (CSP Daily News, 2021). In addition, Walmart, Virgin Atlantic and Duane Reade are all considering implementing the Shopkick technology (Slade, 2014). Additional clients listed on the company's website are 3M, Duracell, The Home Depot, Best Buy, Coca-Cola, H&M, L'Oreal, P&G, TJ Maxx, Marshalls, Sam's Club and Nestle. The third developer of audio beacon technologies, Silverpush, has recently partnered with the marketing firm Digital Commons, in New Zealand, to be implemented in videos. This will result in tracking individuals' TV viewing habits.

Surveillance and Power

As seen from this long list of well-known companies, the clients of audio beacon technologies range from retail, to automotive, to banks, tech companies, airlines and other industries. The rising trend of incorporating these invasive technologies is alarming, especially when we take into consideration their opaque surveillance faculty. As such, audio beacon technologies are becoming an integral part of an emerging web of surveillance and permitting the elimination of previously targeted surveillance practices. Venier and Mordini (as cited in Friedewald et al., 2013) address soft biometric technologies (speech and voice identification) and their privacy implications. Researchers argue that these auditory technologies can be used not only for identification but also for *categorization* of people. Categorization of individuals has ethical implications and consequences because "it constitutes an intervention in the social world of those classified" (Lyon, 2001, p. 173).

Audio surveillance technologies, because they are covert, can be used habitually to aggregate personal data and to map out individual behavior. According to Venier and Mordini (as cited in Friedewald et al., 2013, p. 16), this can lead to generating classification of normal and abnormal behavior. Friedewald et al. (2013) further observe that audio surveillance can be used for automated surveillance on desired topics as well as particular individuals. Other researchers agree with Venier and Mordini, that the danger is not identification of individuals, but rather their categorization. Once the data is aggregated and analyzed, it becomes an essential component of the individual, and the digital profile becomes the foundation for future judgments (Friedewald et al., 2013, pp. 17, 20).

Audio beacon technologies, with their inherent feature of audio transmission, allow for the recording of sonically expressed thoughts and feelings. This data feed can be combined with predictive algorithms and thus reveal a comprehensive digital portrait of individuals. This can be used for commercial reasons today, but the accumulation of data and the ability to be saved for secondary purposes allow the same data to be employed for opportunistic purposes in the future. According to David Lyon (2001), surveillance companies should be held accountable, because the use of personal data affects real human beings (p. 180). Further, the data accumulation is not restricted to targeted individuals, but is an inherent feature of audio beacons, thus allowing mass surveillance of lawful individuals.

Foucault (1980) elucidates that the history of oppression in the 18th and early 19th centuries was a watershed moment when those in power realized that surveillance over the people was more efficient and profitable than public punishment (p. 38). To Foucault, new information creates new knowledge, and this power-knowledge system necessitates each other. If we analyze audio beacons in terms of generating data, then the extraction of personal data can be studied as a form of a concealed power. According to Foucault (1980), if surveillance and accompanying predictability algorithms cease to exist, the powerful would lose their power. John Havens (2016) concurs that the life force of control through an imbalance of power is sustained by complete ignorance of the people and how their data is being used. If individuals were aware of the information being aggregated and its usage, the power would shift back to them. Their refusal to relinquish data or not would shift the power paradigm irreversibly. As users are not consulted beforehand, the obvious conclusion is that the data being collected is of no benefit to the people (Havens, 2016, p. 195). Rudolph Rummel (2017) warns of this grave situation. In his book, *Death by Government*, Rummel (2017) writes that the murders committed by authoritarian regimes can be compared with death counts during war. Killings committed by non-democratic governments are a major cause of human casualties during 20th-century wars. Non-democratic governments commit genocide against dissident groups and their own citizens, which Rummel (2017) labels "democide" (p. 1). He concludes that non-democratic governments are more lethal than wars. Rummel (2017) finds that power is a mandatory prerequisite to commit democide and absolute power breeds violence.

The Digital Paradox Society

The beginning of the 21st century presents us with a paradox. On one hand, we are free to explore online, read various interpretations on any subject, express our opinions and exchange ideas liberally with anyone we choose. On the other side, our actions are surveilled, our data is aggregated and we are subject to behavior manipulation. Many of the privacy and surveillance challenges faced today did not occur as a result of coercion but rather in the course of voluntary activities that are casually enjoyed as entertainment and the consumerist behaviors of everyday life. Contemporary digital society incorporates mass surveillance and new forms of entertainment and consuming intertwined in a paradoxical relationship. To better envision this paradigm, I will juxtapose two masterpieces of modern dystopian literature: Aldous Huxley's *Brave New World* and George Orwell's *Nineteen Eighty-Four*. This approach is relevant today as "the line between science and science fiction is continually redrawn" (Marx, 1998, p. 171).

Consumertainment Surveillance

Examining the complimentary *Nineteen Eighty-Four* and *Brave New World* themes presents a new type of surveillance found in contemporary societies. This surveillance praises the collection of private information, marketed through various channels of popular culture and social media. A surveillance that combines entertainment and consumerism all in one. I call it *consumertainment surveillance*. Administrative surveillance is present in all establishments today (Haggerty & Ericson, 2000, p. 618). Private businesses not only normalize the surveillance state, but they are also making it entertaining. This kind of surveillance glorifies the collection of private information and is popularized by social media, movies and TV shows. Haggerty and Ericson (2000) show how Closed-Circuit TV footage is used for entertainment purposes in TV shows (p. 616), a trend that culminates in the show *Big Brother* where participants are watched 24/7. This mode of entertainment reduces the impact of mass surveillance by turning it into voyeuristic amusement (Giroux, 2015b, p. 113). Consumertainment surveillance inverts the previous convention that spying on law-abiding citizens is done for the purpose of national security and is a procedure reserved for authoritarian regimes (Giroux, 2015b, pp. 113–114). Consumertainment surveillance and its accompanying desire for market share and celebrity-seeking status have made surveillance an accepted form of performance (Giroux, 2015b, p. 115). Thus, consumertainment surveillance has reduced the loss of privacy from a violation to an annoyance in the course of the individual's participation in the consumer lifestyle (Giroux, 2015b, p. 111).

Today's consumertainment surveillance is characterized by several aspects. It involves innumerable actors-agents present in the social media environment (Scolari, 2015, p. 1105). This new environment allows its participants to virtually and instantaneously interact with each other through various fan-based sites, blogs or comment sections. Consumertainment surveillance enables users to self-market themselves. This often happens through sharing personal content, feelings and situations. The main innovation of consumertainment surveillance is target advertising, which is the marketing of goods to users based on their viewing habits. This system involves various algorithms acting as an intermediary between the buyer and the seller. It incorporates different "content providers, affiliate sites, search engines, portals, internet service providers and software makers" (Carr, 2000, p. 46). This mode of advertising provides revenue for countless companies positioned between the viewer and the "entertaining" content. Consumertainment surveillance incorporates various surveillance techniques—eye tracking, auditory surveillance, content viewing, cross-site and cross-device tracking. As observed in the section exploring the audio beacon capabilities, they contribute to the consumertainment surveillance paradigm. Therefore, consumertainment surveillance has a couple of consequences: (1) the daily need for attention reduces individuality to short-lived, narcissistic displays and (2) the complete and voluntary aggregation of all individual activities eliminates the need for the unnecessary exhibition of power (Giroux, 2015b, p. 112).

9.2 Both Sides of the Same Coin

In Huxley's *Brave New World*, members of society are indifferent to the social paradigm because they are too busy experiencing pleasure. The recipe for happiness in Huxley's world is endless consumerism aided by a pharmacological compound called soma. Consumerism and escapism are the basis of society and every bad feeling or unpleasant notion is cured by the soma pill. Soma is given to the population for free and by taking the pill, an individual can escape reality by eliminating pain and anxiety. Orwell's *Nineteen Eighty-Four* shows a dystopian society that is under the ruling of a fictitious figure called Big Brother. He sees and hears all aspects of human behavior through various technological apparitions, which allow the government to control the feelings, desires and aspirations of all the citizens.

Huxley's *Brave New World* does not address mass surveillance and conversely, Orwell's *Nineteen Eighty-Four* omits entertainment. Given these blind spots in the two projected futures, I suggest that the contemporary social order is best analyzed and reflected upon using a combination of Orwell's and Huxley's visions. In the context of audio beacons, a significant similarity between Huxley's and Orwell's worlds is that microphones play a significant role within the surveillance apparatus of the state. In *Nineteen Eighty-Four*, they are used to capture the inner feelings of Winston and Julia. In *Brave New World*, microphones are used to spy on John (the Savage) and to capture his internal state.

The idea of regarding both visions of authoritarian regimes as complimentary is not a new one. According to Henry Giroux (2015a), both books work together to examine current authoritarian tendencies in the United States. The fictional worlds of Orwell and Huxley present opposite environments, but are equally concerned with power. Both societies are completely dominated by the ruling party, but their execution takes different routes. If we combine these two visions of totalitarian society, we recognize the two faces of contemporary society. On one side, we have a power imbalance enhanced by digital algorithms which is reminiscent of Orwell's vision. On the other side, we have consumertainment surveillance, reminiscent of Huxley's vision. Entertainment offers distraction for individuals and shifts the point-of-view away from surveillance practices. Consumertainment surveillance nourishes a state where an "army of managers control[s] a population of slaves who do not have to be coerced, because they love their servitude" (Huxley, 1969, p. xv). Without consumertainment surveillance, the system will collapse and it will resemble Orwell's world with its gaudy display of power.

The Digital Paradox

Contemporary society has its roots in the previous discipline society, as seen from Foucault's (1995) description of the utopian legal penalty system—"deprive the prisoner of all rights, but do not inflict pain; impose penalties free of all pain" (p. 11). According to Foucault (1995), the system focuses on gathering information not about the past, but rather on current activities that provide additional insights revealing their potential for committing future crimes (p. 126). In this penal system, punishment is carried out to transform the criminal, while in the digital paradox, behavior modification is targeted toward mercantile goals. This aspect of surveillance has ethical implications, because it's related to altering an individual's behavior (Nagenborg, 2014, p. 44). As Michael Nagenborg (2014) argues, the ethical assessment of surveillance systems should address "the tension between persuasion and freedom" (p. 44).

For Foucault, an integral part of the disciplinary process emerges from meticulous records of individuals' habits. The emergence of fusion centers, where different types of data are linked to reveal the full digital identity of a person, takes this idea one step further. According to Foucault, this process obscures its own manifestation, prohibiting the individual's involvement. In the digital paradox society, this is ensured by the proprietary nature of data and the absence of disclosure of how algorithms work, what information they gather and how this information is used. The elimination of interference from outside forces succeeds by the scarcity of government legislation. In the digital paradox today two types of protections, constitutional law and regulatory law, have "learned how to use the other's laws to bypass their own restrictions" (Schneier, 2013). The result is the denial of privacy protection through a hidden process that masks personal harm. Citizens can be covertly penalized within an imposed social order of totalitarian measures.

To ensure the order's disciplinary power over the individual, Foucault (1995) observes that the visibility of the populace is paramount—"their visibility assures the hold of the power that is exercised over them" (p. 187). However, in the digital paradox society, the presence of power does not need to be overtly demonstrated. The exercise of power is masked by on-demand entertainment, games and instant-gratification commercialism. In this way, I argue that today's society is a combination of both dystopian and utopian tendencies mixed in a digital paradox. On one hand, we are subjected to penetrating tracking practices that make Orwell's vision of surveillance seem simplistic (Haggerty & Ericson, 2000, p. 612). On the other hand, we are inundated by technologies that help us, make our lives convenient and allay boredom. In Orwell's (1950) quote from *Nineteen Eighty-Four*—"If you want a picture of the future, imagine a boot stamping on a human face—forever" (p. 267), the "boot stamping on a human face" (p. 267) is a symbol for the completely surveilled and oppressed society. In the digital paradox society, with its consumertainment surveillance, Orwell's symbol of surveillance and oppression, the boot, has morphed into Huxley's method of control, soma. In fact, the discernible aspects of the contemporary digital environment astonish us with their variety, usability and lightheartedness. Reminiscent of characters in Huxley's *Brave New World*, we need our daily ration of the custom-designed advertisement popping up at the right moment to fill the gap between loneliness and desire. This accords with Foucault's idea of how discipline over the body can function—it increases utility and concurrently decreases political disobedience (Foucault, 1995, p. 138). In digital paradox societies such as ours, extraordinary measures to protect individual privacy are not only desirable but also imperative.

Mitigating the Surveillance Effect

David Harvey (2019) observes that the state conceptualizes people by their names and bodies. In other words, the state views people as things. He argues that this conceptualization model does not match the actual life of the individual because living life is a process. In that sense, it matters if we continue to generate data, because the process of the continuous generation of data helps conceptualize humans as individuals, where a person is the sum of their digital traces and not an individual of flesh and blood. There are three types of actions to mitigate the mass surveillance tracking by audio beacon technologies: individual actions, self-regulation and government legislation.

Individual Actions

Privacy is both transactional and relational. It is transactional, as it relies on a simple system of allowing access to personal data (or not). It is relational, as in the act of sharing information, one can also inadvertently share the information of others. Collateral data sharing from audio beacons might involve a person's tone of voice, psychological condition and the content of conversations. The creation of audio beacon technologies may have originated from a commercial desire for market share and wealth, but the risk of their realization is detrimental to the populace. The acute remedy is personal accountability. We have denial privileges for every app on our devices and can turn off microphone access. Many apps do not require the microphone to serve the needs of consumers. This one simple action will minimize the cog in the machine of data aggregation and result in a wider social impact.

Self-Regulation

The second option of mitigation falls on corporations to self-regulate their actions of collecting data and to build products that are privacy oriented. Rodrigues et al. (2013) explore the practice of distributing privacy seals by private companies certifying that another company complies with a specific privacy criterion through self-regulation. These seals are designed to ensure users of the enhanced privacy practices of said organization. Researchers conclude that companies issuing privacy seals have a conflict of interest as they are dependent on the funds received from these certified companies. This contradiction leads to an opposing outcome.

Government Legislation

In the course of daily operations, governments are empowered to enforce the rule of law, yet the law has to guarantee the protection of the citizens against the government (Dumortier & Goemans, 2003, p. 5). It is a conundrum—we protect our privacy from the government and simultaneously require the government to quash intrusions of our privacy from others (Hirshleifer, 1980, p. 651).

This state leaves individuals with two meaningful measures—individual action and lobbying local government officials. The former will have an immediate consequence for individuals' data transmission. The latter offers a more robust solution, yet possibly taking longer to carry out. The immediate action of refusing microphone permission in all apps that do not require it would mitigate audio data collection. Concerning location data, individuals can refuse location permission to apps they do not need. In communication apps that require audio, video and text data, users can choose Signal–Private Messenger and Proton. Signal-Private Messenger is a communications app that does not collect, store or share personal information. Proton is a privacy-oriented company that provides email, calendar, VPN and cloud storage. Both of these open-source companies do not share data with third parties or possess the decryption key to read users encrypted communications.

The overall purpose of this research is to raise public awareness of audio beacons, their surveillance capabilities and the connected ethical implications. Simultaneously, this research is hoping to encourage individuals to contact governmental representatives and lobby for better privacy laws protecting consumers. This tactic may be more time consuming, but it is the clear-cut solution to rampant commercially driven surveillance practices using audio beacon technologies. Privacy legislation will improve the long-term protection of individuals. The government as a social institution is tasked with the well-being of its citizens; therefore, privacy legislation will mitigate opportunistic corporate practices engaged only for mercantile reasons.

References

Arp, D., Quiring, E., Wressnegger, C., & Rieck, K. (2017). Privacy threats through ultrasonic side channels on mobile devices. *2017 IEEE European Symposium on Security and Privacy (EuroS&P)*, *4*, 35–47.

Ashbrook, D., & Starner, T. (2003). Using GPS to learn significant locations and predict movement across multiple users. *Personal and Ubiquitous Computing*, *7*, 275–286.

Botin-Sanabria, D. M., Mihaita, A., Piembert-Garcia, R. E., Ramirez-Moreno, M. A., Ramirez-Mendoza, R. A., & Lozoya-Santos, J. (2022). Digital twin technology challenges and applications: A comprehensive review. *Remote Sensing*, *14*(1335), 1–26.

Butler, C. (2019, November). Visa makes strategic investment in LISNR, a start-up that wants to rival technology used by Apple Pay. *CNBC*. www.cnbc.com/2019/11/05/visa-invests-in-lisnr-a-start-up-that-wants-to-rival-apple-pay.html

Carr, N. G. (2000). Hypermediation: Commerce as clickstream. *Harvard Business Review*, *78*(1), 46–48.

Cohen, J. E. (2008). Privacy, visibility, transparency, and exposure. *The University of Chicago Law Review*, *75*(1), 181–201.

Crocco, M., Cristani, M., Trucco, A., & Murino, V. (2016). Audio surveillance: A systematic review. *ACM Computing Surveys*, *48*(4), 1–46, Article 52.

Deleuze, G. (1992, Winter). Postscript on the societies of control. *October*, *59*, 3–7.

Dumortier, J., & Goemans, C. (2003). *Roadmap for European legal research in privacy and identify management* (pp. 1–27). European Commission, DG Information Society, IST Programme, RAPID Project.

ExxonMobil partners with shopkick. (2012, April 3). *CSP Daily News*. Retrieved May 21, 2021, from www.cspdailynews.com/technologyservices/exxonmobil-partners-shopkick

Flynn, K. (2014, July 30). With beacons and audio, LISNR uses proximity marketing to amplify listeners. *Forbes*. www.forbes.com/sites/kerryflynn2014/07/30/with-beacons-and-audio-lisnr-uses-proximity-marketing-to-amplify-listeners/

Foucault, M. (1980). *Power/knowledge: Selected interviews and other writings 1972–1977*. Harvester Press.

Foucault, M. (1995). *Discipline and punish: The birth of the prison*. Vintage Books.

Friedewald, M., Wright, D., & Finn, R. L. (2013, January). *Seven types of privacy* (pp. 1–26). Springer Science+Business Media.

Galic, M., Timan, T., & Koops, B. (2017). Bentham, Deleuze and beyond: An overview of surveillance theories from the panopticon to participation. *Philosophy & Technology*, *30*, 9–37.

Giroux, H. A. (2015a, June 30). Orwell, Huxley and the scourge of the surveillance state. *Truthout*. https://truthout.org/articles/orwell-huxley-and-the-scourge-of-the-surveillance-state/

Giroux, H. A. (2015b). Totalitarian paranoia in the post-orwellian surveillance state. *Cultural Studies*, *29*(2), 108–140.

Haggerty, K. D., & Ericson, R. V. (2000). The surveillant assemblage. *British Journal of Sociology*, *51*(4), 605–622.

Harvey, D. (2019). *Education, part 1, reading Marx's "capital": Vol. 1 with David Harvey*. YouTube. www.youtube.com/watch?v=n5vu4MpYgUo

Havens, J. C. (2016). *Heartifical intelligence*. Jeremy P. Tarcher, Penguin.

Heerden, A., Wassenaar, D., Essack, Z., Vilakazi, K., & Kohrt, B. A. (2019). In-home passive sensor data collection and its implications for social media research: Perspectives of community women in rural South Africa. *Journal of Empirical Research on Human Research Ethics*, *1*(11), 1–11.

Hirshleifer, J. (1980). Privacy: Its origins, function, and nature. *The Journal of Legal Studies*, *9*(4), 649–664.

Huxley, A. (1969). *Brave new world*. Harper & Row.

Lyon, D. (2001). Facing the future: Seeking ethics for everyday surveillance. *Ethics and Information Technology*, *3*, 171–181.

Marx, G. T. (1998). Ethics for the new surveillance. *The Information Society*, *14*, 171–185.

Mavroudis, V., Hao, S., Fratantonio, Y., Maggi, F., Kruegel, C., & Vigna, G. (2017). On the privacy and security of the ultrasound ecosystem. *Proceedings on Privacy Enhancing Technologies*, *2*, 95–112.

Nagenborg, M. (2014). Surveillance and persuasion. *Ethics and Information Technology*, *16*, 43–49.

Orwell, G. (1950). *Nineteen eighty-four*. Signet Classics.

Reddy, S. M. S., Nathwani, K., & Hegde, R. M. (2014). Probabilistic detection methods for acoustic surveillance using audio histograms. *Springer Science+Business Media*, *34*, 1977–1992.

Rehbock, B. (2017, May 30). Jaguar Land Rover partners with LISNR to control cars with sound. *Automobilemag*. www.automobilemag.com/news/jaguar-land-rover-partners-lisnr-control-cars-sound/

Rodrigues, R., Wright, D., & Wadhwa, K. (2013). Developing a privacy seal scheme (that works). *International Data Privacy Law*, *3*(2), 100–116.

Rummel, R. J. (2017). *Death by government*. Routledge.

Schneier, B. (2013, July 13). The public-private surveillance partnership. *Bloomberg*. www.bloomberg.com/opinion/articles/2013-07-31/the-public-privatesurveillance partnership

Scolari, C. A. (2015). From (new)media to (hyper)mediations: Recovering Jesus Martín-Barbero's mediation theory in the age of digital communication and cultural convergence. *Information, Communication & Society*, *18*(9), 1092–1107.

Shopkick. (2021, May 21). *Forbes*. Retrieved May 21, 2021, from www.forbes.com/companies/shopkick/

Slade, H. (2014, July 2). The $30M app that rewards you for just browsing. *Forbes*. www.forbes.com/sites/hollieslade/2014/07/02/the-30m-app-that-rewards-you-for-just-browsing/

Stark, L. (2016). The emotional context of information privacy. *The Information Society*, *32*(1), 14–27.

Sullins, J. (2010). Rights and computer ethics. In L. Floridi (Ed.), *The Cambridge handbook of information and computer ethics* (pp. 116–132). Cambridge University Press.

Taslima, K. (2014, June 22). It all adds up: Silverpush's technology lets advertisers reach the consumers on multiple devices. It could disrupt digital advertising, but will face stiff competition from global pioneers. *Business Today*, 106–108.

Tufekci, Z. (2014). Engineering the public: Big data, surveillance and computational politics. *First Monday*, *19*(7), 3–37.

Vaghasiya, N., Ramoliya, K., Soni, K., & Bhatt, M. (2018, January 5). Mobile based trigger system using near ultrasonic waves. *2018 International Conference of Smart City and Emerging Technology*, 413–419.

Van der Velden, L. (2015). Leaky apps and data shots: Technologies of leakage and insertion in NSA-surveillance. *Surveillance & Society*, *13*(2), 182–196.

West, S. (2019). Data capitalism: Redefining the logics of surveillance and privacy. *Business & Society*, *58*(1), 20–41.

Zittrain, J. (2014, June 3). Facebook could decide an election without anyone ever finding out. *Newstateman*. www.newstatesman.com/politics/2014/06/facebook-could-decide-election-without-anyone-ever-finding-out

Zuboff, S. (2015). Big other: Surveillance capitalism and the prospects of an information civilization. *Journal of Information Technology*, *30*, 75–89.

Index